Library of Congress Cataloging-in-Publication Data
Geisler, Norman L.
    Miracles and the modern mind: a defense of biblical miracles/
Norman L. Geisler.
        p.   cm.
    Rev. ed. of: Miracles and modern thought. 1982.
    Includes bibliographical references.
    ISBN 0–8010–3847–2
    1, Miracles. I. Geisler, Norman L. Miracles and modern thought.
II. Title.
    BT97.2.G44   1991
    231.7'3—dc20
                                                          92–4996

Unless otherwise noted, all Scripture references are from the Holy Bible:
New International Version. Copyright 1983 by the International Bible
Society. Used by permission of Zondervan Bible Publishers.

MIRACLES
AND THE MODERN MIND

MIRACLES
AND THE MODERN MIND

A Defense
of Biblical Miracles

NORMAN L. GEISLER

BAKER BOOK HOUSE
Grand Rapids, Michigan 49516

CONTENTS

ACKNOWLEDGMENTS

I WISH TO EXPRESS my thanks to several people who helped in preparing this manuscript: Thomas Howe, Sharon Coomer, Terri Hayden, and Renée Willard. Their assistance is greatly appreciated. Also, much of the material used here appeared in an earlier form in *Miracles and Modern Thought* (Probe, 1982). The present work has completely revised, updated, and extensively supplemented this unobtainable material.

INTRODUCTION

CONTEMPORARY ATTITUDES TOWARD MIRACLES embrace two extremes. On the one hand, secular skeptics reject miracles outright. The scientific community, for example, has been dominated for two centuries by an incorrigible antisupernaturalism. Many insist that belief in the supernatural is part of an outmoded worldview that has been disproved by scientific research. Biblical miracles are classed along with the now discredited belief that tornadoes, hurricanes, eclipses, and earthquakes were miraculous because they could not be explained scientifically.

Typical of the scientific attitude toward the supernatural is the decision of Judge William Overton in the famous Scopes II trial in Little Rock, Arkansas: "Indeed, creation of the world 'out of nothing' is the ultimate religious statement because God is the only actor. . . . Such a concept is not science because it depends upon supernatural intervention which is not guided by natural law. It is not explanatory by reference to natural law, is not testable and is not falsifiable."[1] A recent *Smithsonian* article characterizes the scientific distaste for the supernatural view of origins: "the central axiom of our epic is that the universe must have been formed by natural laws which are still discoverable today."[2]

The author of the Declaration of Independence, Thomas Jefferson, reflects the antisupernatural disposition of the modern mind when he declares of the virgin birth that "The day will come when the account of the birth of Christ as accepted in the Trinitarian churches will be classed with the fable of Minerva springing from the brain of Jupiter."[3]

1. See Norman L. Geisler, *The Creator in the Courtroom* (Grand Rapids: Baker, 1982), pp. 174, 176.
2. James S. Trefil, "Closing in on Creation," *Smithsonian* 14/2 (May 1983): 33.
3. Henry Wilder Foote, *Thomas Jefferson* (Boston: Beacon, 1947), p. 49.

Some contemporary antisupernaturalists share Sigmund Freud's view that belief in the supernatural is a form of escapism or an illusion. Religion is dismissed as a childhood neurosis that people use to protect themselves from the horrible realities of life. Ludwig Feuerbach contends that belief in the supernatural saps needed human energy from this world. His aim is "to change the friends of God into friends of man, believers into thinkers, worshippers into workers, candidates for the other world into students of this world, Christians, who on their own confession are half animal and half angel, into men—whole men."[4]

On the opposite extreme, there is a current revival of occult "supernaturalism" in new age healings, revelations, firewalking, and crystal power. Many gurus, channelers, mediums, shamans, and witches lay claim to the supernormal power of the Force. The famous Hindu guru, Sai Baba, boasts: "My power is divine and has no limit. I have the power to change the earth into the sky and the sky into the earth. . . . I am beyond any obstacles and there is no force, natural or supernatural, that can stop me or my mission."[5]

A growing number of evangelicals believe that miraculous healings and even resurrections like those in the Bible still occur today. They make claims like "Today we see hundreds of people healed every month in Vineyard Christian Fellowship services. Many more are healed as we pray for them in hospitals, on the streets, and in homes. The blind see; the lame walk; the deaf hear. Cancer is disappearing."[6]

Whatever the outcome of the intramural dispute among Christians about the status of miracles today,[7] the whole question of the supernatural has a serious impact on biblical Christians of all stripes. For historic evangelical Christianity is at its heart thoroughly based in the Scripture, which is filled with miraculous events. Indeed, the Bible itself cannot be a supernatural revelation, as it claims to be, unless there are supernatural acts. Neither can we trust the Gospels to provide reliable information about Christ, the central figure of the Christian faith, since they are replete with miraculous events repugnant to the modern mind.

4. Quoted by Karl Barth, "An Introductory Essay" to Ludwig Feuerbach, *The Essence of Christianity* (New York: Harper and Row, 1957), p. xi.

5. Tal Brooke, *The Lord of the Air* (Eugene, Oreg.: Harvest House, 1990), p. 214.

6. John Wimber, *Power Evangelism* (New York: Harper and Row, 1986), p. 44.

7. We have addressed this issue elsewhere. See Norman L. Geisler, *Signs and Wonders* (Wheaton: Tyndale, 1988).

Indeed, since the credibility of Christianity rests on the resurrection of Christ (1 Cor. 15:12–19), the whole of the orthodox Christian faith crumbles if miracles do not occur. If historic biblical Christianity is to survive and make sense to the modern mind, it is necessary to provide a reasonable explanation of the supernatural. Apart from the credibility of the biblical account of miracles, we can bid farewell to orthodox Christianity. Such is the challenge before us.

 **1**

ARE MIRACLES IMPOSSIBLE?

I use the word *miracle* to mean an interference with Nature by
supernatural power.—C. S. Lewis

THE BIBLICAL RECORD is replete with miraculous stories. Moses
stretched out his hand over the waters and the Red Sea divided. The
sun stopped in the middle of the sky for a whole day. Elisha made
an iron axe float on the water. Jesus gave sight to the blind, caused
the lame to walk, and raised his friend Lazarus from the dead. He
walked on water, turned water into wine, and multiplied a few loaves
and some fish into food for five thousand people. This is the world
of the Bible. It is a world of unusual and miraculous events—and a
world almost totally foreign to the modern mind.

The modern scientific world, by contrast, is a natural one. It is a
world in which solid metal objects heavier than water sink, as do
people who step into water. It is a world in which water flows to its
own level but does not form vertical walls. It is a world where the
dead remain in the grave and where winemakers cannot fill their
wine barrels from the water faucet; they must wait for slow natural
processes to produce wine from grapes. Indeed, the biblical world
and the modern world are worlds apart. The one seems mythical and
the other real. The one seems superstitious and the other scientific.

Before we consider miracles and the modern mind, we must first
investigate the term "miracle." As Thomas Huxley has pointed out,
"The first step in this, as in all other discussions, is to come to a clear
understanding as to the meaning of the term employed.
Argumentation about whether miracles are possible and, if possible,

13

credible, is mere beating the air until the arguers have agreed what they mean by the word 'miracle.'"[1]

Theists have defined miracles in either a weak or a strong sense. Following Augustine, some define a miracle as "a portent [that] is not contrary to nature, but contrary to our knowledge of nature."[2] Others, following Aquinas, define a miracle in the strong sense of an event that is beyond nature's power to produce, that only a supernatural power (God) can do. This latter sense is the meaning of miracle as used in this book. In brief, a miracle is a divine intervention into the natural world. It is a supernatural exception to the regular course of the world that would not have occurred otherwise. As Antony Flew puts it, "A miracle is something which would never have happened had nature, as it were, been left to its own devices."[3] Natural law describes naturally caused regularities; a miracle is a supernaturally caused singularity.

In order to expand on the meaning of the term "miracle," we need some initial understanding of what is meant by natural law. Natural law can be understood as the usual, orderly, and general way that the world operates. It follows, then, that a miracle is an unusual, irregular, specific way in which God acts within the world. As Sir George Stokes, the famous physicist who discovered the laws that now bear his name, has said, "It may be that the event which we call a miracle was brought about not by the suspension of the laws in ordinary operation, but by the super-addition of something not ordinarily in operation."[4] In other words, if a miracle occurs, it would not be a violation or contradiction of the ordinary laws of cause and effect, but rather a new effect produced by the introduction of a supernatural cause.

Keeping this definition of miracles in mind, we will examine the most important philosophers in the miracles debate of the last three hundred years. We do this in order to get a closer look at the reasons why it is so difficult for most thinking persons to maintain a serious belief in the supernatural. One of the reasons for this difficulty emanates from the philosophy of the famous seventeenth-century Jewish philosopher Benedict Spinoza (1632–1677). Arguing from a strongly deductive perspective, this Dutch Jewish thinker did not hesitate to pronounce the belief in miracles absurd.

1. Thomas Huxley, *The Works of T. H. Huxley* (New York: Appleton, 1896), p. 153.
2. Augustine, *City of God* 21.8.
3. Antony Flew, "Miracles," in *The Encyclopedia of Philosophy*, ed. Paul Edwards (New York: Macmillan, 1967), 5:346.
4. As quoted in the *International Standard Bible Encyclopedia* (Grand Rapids: Eerdmans, 1939), p. 2063.

Benedict Spinoza and the Impossibility of Miracles

Spinoza was one of the early rationalists, a gifted and brilliant philosopher who developed a complete form of pantheism. A lens-grinder by trade, Spinoza was so original and unorthodox in his thinking that his views caused him to be expelled from the Jewish synagogue when he was only twenty-four years of age. Spinoza believed that there could be only one infinite substance, and that therefore the universe was uncreated. In other words, God is identical with the universe. He could not have created it, for it is of his essence. God is not transcendent; he is not beyond or "other" than creation. This means, then, that God's creativity is no more than nature's activity. Miracles, therefore, are impossible. For if God (the supernatural) is identical to nature, then it follows that there is no supernatural intervention into nature from anything beyond it.

The Character of Spinoza's Argument

Spinoza declares that "nothing . . . comes to pass in nature in contravention to her universal laws, nay, everything agrees with them and follows from them, for . . . she keeps a fixed and immutable order." In fact, "a miracle, whether in contravention to, or beyond, nature, is a mere absurdity." Spinoza is dogmatic when it comes to the impossibility of miracles. He unashamedly proclaims that "We may, then, be absolutely certain that every event which is truly described in Scripture necessarily happened, like everything else, according to natural laws."[5]

Spinoza's argument against miracles can be reduced to some basic premises:

1. Miracles are violations of natural laws.
2. Natural laws are immutable.
3. It is impossible to violate immutable laws.
4. Therefore, miracles are impossible.

The second premise is the key to Spinoza's argument. Nature "keeps a fixed and *immutable* order."[6] Everything "*necessarily* happened . . . according to natural laws."[7] Spinoza believes that "noth-

5. Benedict Spinoza, *A Theologico-Political Treatise*, trans. R. H. M. Elwes (New York: Dover, 1951), 1:83, 87, 92.

6. Ibid., p. 83.

7. Ibid., p. 92, emphasis added.

ing comes to pass in nature in contravention to her [nature's] universal laws."[8] To believe otherwise "is a mere absurdity."[9]

In order to appreciate what Spinoza means, we need to recognize that he was a rationalist who tried to construct his philosophy on the model of Euclid's geometry.[10] He believed that we should accept as true only what is self-evident or what is reducible to the self-evident. Like his French contemporary, René Descartes, Spinoza argued in a geometric way from axioms to conclusions contained in these axioms. Spinoza lived in an age increasingly impressed with the orderliness of the physical universe. Because of this it was axiomatic to Spinoza that natural laws are immutable.

The Consequence of Spinoza's Argument

Spinoza's rationalism has far-reaching consequences for anyone who believes in either miraculous events or supernatural revelations. In point of fact, because of this Spinoza became one of the first modern thinkers to engage in systematic higher criticism of the Bible. His *Theologico-Political Treatise* (1670), widely circulated in the late seventeenth century, was chiefly a critical commentary on the Bible.

First, Spinoza's naturalistic rationalism leads him to conclude that since "there are many passages in the Pentateuch which Moses could not have written, it follows that the belief that Moses was the author of the Pentateuch is ungrounded and even irrational."[11] Who wrote the first five books of the Old Testament? The same person, says Spinoza, who wrote the rest of the Old Testament—Ezra the scribe.[12]

Second, Spinoza rejects the resurrection accounts in the Gospels. Concerning Christianity he notes that "the Apostles who came after Christ, preached it to all men as a universal religion *solely* in virtue of Christ's Passion."[13] In other words, Spinoza reduces Christianity to a mystical, nonpropositional religion, a religion without foundations. Orthodox Christianity has held, since Paul (see 1 Cor. 15:1–14),

8. Ibid., p. 83.
9. Ibid., p. 87.
10. Benedict Spinoza, *Ethics*, ed. James Gutmann (New York: Hafner, 1949), pt. 1, pp. 41–42.
11. Spinoza, *Theologico-Political Treatise*, p. 126.
12. Ibid., pp. 129–30.
13. Ibid., p. 170, emphasis added.

that apart from the truth of the resurrection of Christ, Christianity is a religion without hope.

Third, for Spinoza, the Scripture merely "contains the word of God."[14] In Spinoza's view, it is false to say, as orthodox Christians have, that the Bible *is* the Word of God. Rather the parts of the Bible that contain the word of God are known to be such because the morality contained therein conforms to a natural law known by human reason.[15]

Fourth, Spinoza categorically denies all miracles in the Bible. He commends "anyone who seeks for the true causes of miracles and strives to understand natural phenomena as an intelligent being."[16] Not only does he conclude that "every event . . . in Scripture necessarily happened, like everything else, according to natural laws,"[17] but that Scripture itself "makes the general assertion in several passages that nature's course is *fixed and unchangeable*."[18]

Finally, Spinoza maintains that the prophets did not speak from supernatural "revelation." Moreover, "the modes of expression and discourse adopted by the Apostles in the Epistles, show very clearly that the latter were not written by revelation and Divine command, but *merely by the natural powers* and judgment of the authors."[19]

Not everyone would agree with Spinoza's rationalistic basis for rejecting miracles. Both the spirit of his antisupernaturalism and general criticism of the Bible are, however, still widely held today by both secular and liberal Christian scholars.

An Evaluation of Spinoza's Critique

Spinoza's attack on miracles rests on three foundations: his Euclidean rationalism, his deterministic view of natural laws, and his view of the nature of God. All three foundations have been subject to serious criticism and, as we will see, each falls far short as a definitive argument against miracles.

14. Ibid., p. 165.
15. Ibid., pp. 172, 196–97.
16. Spinoza, *Ethics*, pt. 1, prop. 36, appendix.
17. Spinoza, *Theologico-Political Treatise*, p. 92.
18. Ibid., p. 96, emphasis added.
19. Ibid., p. 159, emphasis added. Spinoza sometimes says that the prophets spoke by revelation, but understands revelation as the "extraordinary power . . . [of] the imagination of the prophets" (ibid., p. 24).

Spinoza's Deductive Deck Is Stacked

Spinoza's Euclidean (deductive) rationalism suffers from an acute case of *petitio principii* (begging the question). For, as David Hume notes, anything validly deducible from premises must have already been present in those premises from the beginning. But if the anti-supernatural is already presupposed in Spinoza's rationalistic premises, then it is no surprise to discover him attacking the miracles of the Bible.

What is really at stake is the truth of the rationalistic premises for which Spinoza has provided no convincing argument, not even one persuasive for most other naturalists. In other words, once we define natural laws as "fixed," "immutable," and "unchangeable," then of course it is irrational to say a miracle occurred. How can anything break the unbreakable?

Spinoza's God and Modern Science

Spinoza's view of God is pantheistic. God and the universe are of one substance; God is coterminous with nature. Hence, a miracle as an act of a God beyond nature cannot occur. Indeed, miracles as supernatural interventions are possible only in a theistic universe. Hence, scientists will want reasons to believe that a theistic God exists before they are likely to believe there is any evidence for miracles. In Spinoza's monastically tight concept of nature (= God), there is simply no room for miracles.

Albert Einstein's belief in Spinoza's God gave rise to one of the more fascinating stories in modern science. The highly respected astrophysicist Robert Jastrow tells of the reluctance of scientists to conclude that the universe came into existence with a "Big Bang" some alleged billions of years ago. Jastrow offers several lines of scientific evidence that support a beginning of the universe: the fact that the universe is running down (and thus cannot be eternal), Einstein's theory of relativity, and the fact that the universe is expanding from its original explosion (even the radiation "echo" of the original explosion has allegedly been discovered). The discovery of the radiation "echo," writes Jastrow, "has convinced almost the last doubting Thomas."[20] Concerning this, he continues, "theologians generally are delighted with the proof that the universe had a beginning, but astronomers are curiously upset."[21]

20. Robert Jastrow, *God and the Astronomers* (New York: Norton, 1978), p. 15.
21. Ibid., p. 16.

A most notable example of how scientists become upset at these findings is the case of Einstein. Einstein developed the general theory of relativity but failed to observe that an expanding universe followed as a conclusion from his own theory. Russian mathematician Alexander Friedmann pointed out that Einstein's failure to conclude that the universe had a beginning came about because he "had made a schoolboy error in algebra."[22] In effect, he had divided by zero! What did the scientific genius Einstein do when Friedmann pointed out his error? He defended his thesis by a "proof" that contained yet another mistake! Eventually Einstein recognized his error and wrote, "My objection rested on an error in calculation. I consider Mr. Friedmann's results to be correct and illuminating."[23] However, "this circumstance [of an expanding universe] irritated me." In another place he said, "To admit such possibilities seems senseless."[24]

Why would such a brilliant mathematical mind consider "senseless" the view that the universe had a beginning, and how was he "irritated" into making a simple mathematical error? Part of the answer, says Jastrow, lies in Einstein's philosophical conception of God and the universe. In 1921 a rabbi sent Einstein a telegram asking, "Do you believe in God?" to which Einstein answered, "*I believe in Spinoza's God,* who reveals himself in the orderly harmony of what exists."[25] This explains why Einstein could not believe in a supernatural beginning of the universe. As we have seen, Spinoza was a rationalist for whom God's essence is equated with the universe and for whom the universe is eternal and operates only according to uniform natural law.

Today we have scientific evidence that the universe is of finite age, that it had a beginning. Therefore, for rational minds creation would seem to be the only alternative. Why? As William James points out, "From nothing to being there is no logical bridge."[26] It makes no sense to say, with C. F. von Weizsacker, that all things have come from "nothingness pregnant with being,"[27] since "nothing" means

22. Ibid., p. 25.
23. Ibid., p. 27.
24. Ibid., p. 28.
25. Ibid., emphasis added.
26. William James, *Some Problems of Philosophy* (New York: Longmans, Green, 1911), p. 40.
27. C. F. von Weizsacker, *The Relevance of Science* (New York: Harper and Row, 1964), p. 36.

nonbeing. In view of the increasing evidence, British physicist Edmund Whittaker concludes that "It is simpler to postulate creation *ex nihilo*—divine will constituting Nature from nothingness."[28]

Some have suggested a winding and rewinding process going on forever, but there are several problems with this theory. First, Jastrow points out that the creation (from nothing) of fresh hydrogen atoms is necessary for the "rewinding" process. But contrary to Jastrow's own agnosticism about how this occurred, this would necessitate postulating a God to create them (nothing cannot produce something). Second, others point to the impossibility of having an actual infinite series of events (of "winding" and "unwinding") going backwards, since no matter how many there were, one more could always be added. Potential or abstract (mathematical) infinite series are possible, but not actual, concrete ones. Finally, regardless of whether an infinite series of moments is possible, a universe "bouncing back" in seemingly endless rebounds is a violation of the firmly established Second Law of Thermodynamics. For in a closed, isolated system, such as the universe as a whole is by definition, there is always a loss of usable energy every time there is a collapse or rebound. If the universe is rebounding, it would take longer to run down, but it would not "rebound" as far each time. So no matter what, it would eventually peter out anyway. So, it looks like the universe would run down anyway—it would just take longer.[29]

Despite the strong scientific evidence for a unique point of beginning for the universe, many scientists strongly resist this conclusion. In 1931 Sir Arthur Stanley Eddington wrote, "The expanding universe is preposterous . . . incredible. . . . It leaves me cold."[30] More recently Phillip Morrison of MIT said, "I find it hard to accept the Big Bang theory; I would like to reject it."[31] Even Allan Sandage of Palomar Observatory once said, "It is such a strange conclusion. . . . It cannot really be true."[32] In spite of his earlier acknowledgment of the strong evidence for the Big Bang origin of the universe, even Stephen Hawking is looking for alternatives.[33]

28. Jastrow, *God and the Astronomers*, pp. 111–12.
29. See William Lane Craig, *The Kalam Cosmological Argument* (New York: Macmillan, 1923), pt. 2.
30. Ibid., p. 112.
31. Ibid., p. 113.
32. Ibid.
33. See Stephen Hawking, *A Brief History of Time* (New York: Bantam, 1988).

But, as Jastrow notes, scientists are being upset by their own scientific discoveries. He concludes his book with these vivid words: "For the scientist who has lived by faith in the power of reason, the story ends like a bad dream. He has scaled the mountain of ignorance; he is about to conquer the highest peak; as he pulls himself over the final rock, he is greeted by a band of theologians who have been sitting there for centuries."[34]

Modern philosophy and science since before the so-called Enlightenment cast serious doubt on the traditional belief in miracles. Spinoza was a leader in the attack. But when his arguments are examined carefully, they are found wanting, both in the light of their philosophical presuppositions and in view of the findings of contemporary science.

Spinoza's argument fails because, first, it begs the question by defining miracles as impossible to begin with, namely, as a violation of assumed unbreakable natural laws. What Spinoza needed to do, but did not, was to provide some sound argument for his rationalistic presuppositions. In short, his reasoning is geometric, but his rationalistic "axioms" are wrong. He spins them out in the thin air of rational speculation, but they are never firmly attached to the firm ground of empirical observation.

Second, Spinoza's concept of natural law as a deterministic system is self-defeating. If everything is determined, then so is the view that determinism is wrong. But determinism cannot be both true and false. Thus, Spinoza's basis for antisupernaturalism is unfounded, and miracles cannot be pronounced impossible.

Finally, the evidence has mounted for a unique beginning of the space-time universe. If this is so, then the beginning of the universe would be a prime example of a miracle. What else should we call something coming into existence from nothing? Further, concluding that the universe had a beginning provides a devastating blow to Spinoza's concept of God, and calls into question the naturalistic view that no God exists beyond the natural world. Rather than arguing against miracles, science may be coming back (however reluctantly) to the supernatural.

34. Jastrow, *God and the Astronomers*, p. 116.

2

ARE MIRACLES INCREDIBLE?

> The most incredible thing about miracles is that they happen.—G. K. Chesterton

WHILE FEW CONTEMPORARY THINKERS accept the rationalistic basis from which Spinoza launched his attack on miracles, they have by no means expressed a willingness to return to a pre-Enlightenment belief in the supernatural. Most modern thinkers who reject miracles trace their heritage to the famous Scottish skeptic, David Hume, who has provided what many believe to be the most formidable of all challenges to a supernaturalist perspective.

The Basis for Hume's Critique of Miracles

David Hume (1711–1776) was a philosopher and historian, born and reared in Edinburgh, where he attended Edinburgh University. He later earned a degree in law but soon after decided not to practice. Instead, during the height of the European Enlightenment, Hume took up a rigorous study of philosophy. This study led to skepticism and a disdain for the miraculous. Hume's significance for the study of miracles can be found in his epistemological method and his view of natural law.

Unlike Spinoza, Hume attacked miracles not from a rationalistic perspective but from an empirical one. In many ways the two men were opposites. Spinoza was dogmatic and Hume was a skeptic. Spinoza was rationalistic and Hume was empirical.[1] These differences notwithstand-

---

1. Things known a priori are known *prior to* and *independent of* experience. Things known a posteriori are known *from* (after) experience.

ing, both men maintained that it was unreasonable to believe in miracles. There is, however, an important difference. For Spinoza, miracles are actually impossible; for Hume, they are merely incredible.

Hume's Empirical Skepticism

Hume believes that "all the objects of human reason or inquiry may naturally be divided into two kinds, to wit, 'Relations of Ideas,' and 'Matters of Fact.'"[2] The first kind includes mathematical statements and definitions; the second includes everything known empirically, that is, through one or more of the five senses. So emphatic is Hume about this distinction that he concludes his famous *Inquiry* with these words:

> When we run over libraries, persuaded of these principles, what havoc must we make? If we take in our hand any volume—of divinity or school metaphysics, for instance—let us ask, Does it contain any abstract reasoning concerning quantity or number? No. Does it contain any experimental reasoning concerning matter of fact and existence? No. Commit it then to the flames, for it can contain nothing but sophistry and illusion.[3]

Cause and Effect

For Hume "all reasoning concerning matter of fact seems to be founded on the relation of cause and effect. By means of that relation alone we can go beyond the evidence of our memory and senses."[4] In view of this, the mind can never find the cause for a given event. Only "after the constant conjunction of two objects, heat and flame, for instance . . . we are determined by custom alone to expect the one from the appearance of the other."[5] That is, we make use of causality, but we have no empirical grounds for doing so. In short, we cannot know causal connections between things; we can only believe in them based on customary conjunctions. "All inferences from experience, therefore, are effects of custom, not of reasoning."[6]

According to Hume, we cannot even be sure the sun will rise tomorrow. We can (and do) believe it will, because it has customarily risen in the past. Of course, some things happen so often in con-

2. David Hume, *An Inquiry Concerning Human Understanding*, ed. C. W. Hendel (New York: Bobbs-Merrill, 1955), sec. 4, pt. 1, p. 40.
3. Ibid., 12.3.173.
4. Ibid., 4.1.41.
5. Ibid., 5.1.57.
6. Ibid.

junction with other things that it is foolish not to believe they will be so conjoined in the future. Hume would even call this uniform experience a "proof," by which he means "such arguments from experience as leave no room for doubt or opposition."[7] Nonetheless, "all events seem entirely loose and separate. One event follows another; but we never can observe any tie between them. They seem conjoined, but never connected."[8] But conjoined events do not prove they are causally connected any more than there is a causal connection between the rooster crowing and the sun rising! All we can do is extrapolate based on oft-repeated occurrences.

Hume's Claim: The Incredibility of Miracles

Building on his empirical epistemology, Hume launches his attack on miracles in part 10 of his *Inquiry*.[9] In introducing his argument, Hume comments, "I flatter myself that I have discovered an argument . . . which, if just, will, with the wise and learned, be an everlasting check to all kinds of superstitious delusion, and consequently will be useful as long as the world endures."[10]

A Summary of Hume's Argument Against Miracles

Just what is this "final" argument against miracles? Hume's reasoning is as follows:

1. "A wise man . . . proportions his belief to the evidence."[11]
2. "If such conclusions are founded on an infallible experience, he expects the event with the last degree of assurance and regards his past experience as a full proof of the future existence of that event."[12]
3. "As the evidence derived from witnesses and human testimony is founded on past experience, so it varies with the experience and is regarded either as a proof or a probability, according as the conjunction between any particular

7. Ibid., 6.1.69.
8. Ibid., 7.2.85.
9. Hume actually presents two arguments against miracles here. The first is an argument *in principle*, which assumes the credibility of witnesses. The second is an argument *in practice*, which challenges in fact whether any miracles have ever had credible witnesses.
10. Ibid., 10.1.118.
11. Ibid.
12. Ibid.

kind of report and any kind of object has been found to be
constant or variable."[13]

4. "There are a number of circumstances to be taken into consideration in all judgments of this kind; and the ultimate standard
   by which we determine all disputes that may arise concerning
   them is always derived from experience and observation."[14]

5. "Where this experience is not entirely uniform on any side,
   it is attended with an unavoidable contrariety in our judgments and with the same opposition and mutual destruction
   of argument as in every other kind of evidence."[15]

6. "We entertain a suspicion concerning any matter of fact
   when the witnesses contradict each other, when they are but
   few or of a doubtful character, when they have an interest
   in what they affirm, when they deliver their testimony with
   hesitation or . . . with too violent asseverations."[16]

7. "But when the fact attested is such a one as has seldom
   fallen under our observation, here is a contest of two opposite experiences; of which the one destroys the other as far as
   its force goes, and the superior can only operate on the
   mind by the force which remains."[17]

8. "A miracle is a violation of the laws of nature; and . . . firm
   and unalterable experience has established these laws."[18]

9. Therefore, "the proof against a miracle, from the very
   nature of the fact, is as entire as any argument from experience can possibly be imagined."[19]

10. Since "a uniform experience amounts to a proof, there is
    here a direct and full proof, from the nature of the fact,
    against the existence of any miracle."[20]

Hume's argument can be summarized as follows:

1. A miracle is a violation of the laws of nature.
2. Firm and unalterable experience has established these laws
   of nature.

13. Ibid., 10.1.120.
14. Ibid.
15. Ibid.
16. Ibid.
17. Ibid., 10.1.121.
18. Ibid., 10.1.122.
19. Ibid.
20. Ibid. 10.1.123.

3. Wise individuals proportion belief to the evidence.
4. The proof against miracles is as entire as any argument from experience can possibly be imagined.

Hume concludes that "There must, therefore, be a uniform experience against every miraculous event. Otherwise the event would not merit that appellation." So "nothing is esteemed a miracle if it ever happened in the common course of nature."[21]

Understanding Hume's Argument

There are two basic ways to understand Hume's argument against miracles. We will call these the "hard" and "soft" interpretations.

According to the "hard" interpretation of the argument, Hume would be saying:

1. Miracles by definition are a violation of natural law.
2. Natural laws are unalterably uniform.
3. Therefore, miracles cannot occur.

Despite the fact that Hume's argument sometimes sounds like this, it is not necessarily what he has in mind. If this is his argument, then it clearly begs the question by simply defining miracles as impossible. For if miracles are a "violation" of what cannot be "altered," then miracles are ipso facto impossible. Supernaturalists could easily avoid this dilemma. They could refuse to define miracles as "violations" of fixed law and simply call them "exceptions" to a general rule. That is, they could define natural law as the regular (normal) pattern of events but not as a universal or unalterable pattern.

This would be an easy way out of the problem for supernaturalists. Actually, Hume's position contains an argument that is much more difficult to answer, one that addresses this "softer" view of natural law. It is not an argument for the *impossibility* of miracles but for the *incredibility* of miracles. It can be stated as follows:

1. A miracle is by definition a rare occurrence.
2. Natural law is by definition a description of regular occurrence.
3. The evidence for the regular is always greater than that for the rare.

21. Ibid., 10.1.122–23.

4. Wise individuals always base belief on the greater evidence.
5. Therefore, wise individuals should never believe in miracles.

Note that on this "soft" form of the argument miracles are not ruled out entirely; they are simply held to be always incredible by the very nature of the evidence. Wise people do not claim that miracles cannot occur; they simply never *believe* miracles happen, because they never have enough evidence for that belief. One indication that Hume is stressing credibility (or believability) is found in his use of the terms "belief," "is esteemed," and the like.

Yet even in this "soft" interpretation of the argument, miracles are still eliminated, since by the very nature of the case no thoughtful person should ever hold that a miracle has indeed occurred. If this is so, Hume has seemingly avoided begging the question and yet has successfully eliminated the possibility of reasonable belief in miracles.

Responding to Hume's Arguments Against Miracles

Since the "hard" form of Hume's argument clearly begs the question and is easily answered by redefining the terms, we will concentrate primarily on the "soft" form. In order to proceed, a brief discussion of Hume's claim for uniform experience is necessary.

Uniform Experience

Hume speaks of "uniform" experience in his argument against miracles, but this either begs the question or else is special pleading. It begs the question if Hume presumes to know the experience is uniform in advance of looking at the evidence. For how can we know that all possible experience will confirm naturalism, unless we have access to all possible experiences, including those in the future? If, on the other hand, Hume simply means by "uniform" experience the select experiences of *some* persons (who have not encountered a miracle), then this is special pleading. For there are others who claim to have experienced miracles. As Stanley Jaki observes, "Insofar as he was a sensationist or empiricist philosopher he had to grant equal credibility to the recognition of any fact, usual or unusual."[22]

In the final analysis, the debate over miracles cannot be settled by supposed "uniform" experience. For this either begs the question in advance or else opens the door to a factual analysis of whether

22. Stanley Jaki, *Miracles and Physics* (Front Royal, Va.: Christendom, 1989), p. 23.

indeed there is sufficient evidence to believe that a miracle has occurred. As C. S. Lewis observes,

> Now of course we must agree with Hume that if there is absolutely "uniform experience" against miracles, if in other words they have never happened, why then they never have. Unfortunately we know the experience against them to be uniform only if we know that all the reports of them are false. And we can know all the reports to be false only if we know already that miracles have never occurred. In fact, we are arguing in a circle.[23]

The only alternative to this circular arguing is to be open to the possibility that miracles have occurred.

Furthermore, Hume does not really weigh evidence for miracles; he simply adds evidence against them. Since death occurs over and over and over again and resurrection occurs only on rare occasions, he simply adds up all the deaths against the very few alleged resurrections and rejects the latter. In Hume's own words, "It is no miracle that a man, seemingly in good health, should die on a sudden, because such a kind of death has yet been frequently observed to happen. But it is a miracle that a dead man should come to life; because that has never been observed in any age or country." Hence, "it is more probable that all men must die."[24]

There are other problems with Hume's concept of adding up events to determine truth. First, even if a few resurrections actually occurred, according to Hume's principles we should not believe them, since the number of deaths would always outweigh them. Truth is not, however, determined by majority vote. Hume here commits a kind of *consensus gentium*.[25]

Second, this argument equates "evidence" and "probability." It says in effect that we should always believe what is most probable, that is, what has the highest "odds." On these grounds we should not believe the dice we rolled shows three sixes if we get them on the first roll, since the odds against this happening are 216 to 1. Or we should not believe we were dealt a perfect bridge hand (which has happened) since the odds against this happening are

---

23. C. S. Lewis, *Miracles* (New York: Macmillan, 1969), p. 105.

24. Hume, *Inquiry* 10.1.122. For discussion of Hume's critique of miracles, see Ronald Nash, *Faith and Reason* (Grand Rapids: Zondervan, 1988).

25. A *consensus gentium* is an informal logical fallacy arguing that something is true because it is believed by most people.

1,635,013,559,600 to 1! What Hume overlooks is that wise people base their beliefs on facts, not on odds. Sometimes the "odds" against an event are high (based on past observation), but the evidence for the event is very good (based on current observation or testimony).

Third, Hume's concept of "adding" evidence would eliminate any unusual or unique event from the past, to say nothing of miracles. Richard Whately satirizes Hume's thesis in his famous pamphlet, *Historical Doubts Concerning the Existence of Napoleon Bonaparte*. Since Napoleon's exploits were so fantastic, so extraordinary, so unprecedented, no intelligent person should believe that these events ever happened. After recounting Napoleon's amazing and unparalleled military feats, Whately asks, "Does anyone believe all this and yet refuse to believe a miracle? Or rather, what is this but a miracle? Is not this a violation of the laws of nature?" If skeptics do not deny the existence of Napoleon, they "must at least acknowledge that they do not apply to that question the same plan of reasoning which they have made use of in others."[26]

Finally, Hume's argument proves too much. It proves that we should not believe in a miracle even if it happens! We should not believe miracles have occurred because the evidence for the regular is always greater than that for the rare. But on this logic, if a miracle did occur—rare as it may be—we should still not believe in it. There is something patently absurd about claiming that an event should be disbelieved, even if we know that it has occurred!

Eliminating Belief in Present Events
Based on Evidence for Past Events

It would seem that Hume wants wise people always to believe in advance that miracles will never occur. Even before we examine the evidence, we come "prearmed" with the "uniform" and "unalterable" testimony of the past, so that even if a given event seems highly miraculous, it should not be presumed to be a miracle. Hume even calls it "infallible experience" which provides "the last (i.e., highest) degree of assurance and regards past experience as a full proof of the future existence of that event."[27]

---

26. Richard Whately, *Historical Doubts Concerning the Existence of Napoleon Bonaparte*, in *Famous Pamphlets*, ed. Henry Morley, 2d ed. (London: George Routledge and Sons, 1890), pp. 274, 290.
27. Hume, *Inquiry* 10.1.118.

Once again Hume's uniformitarian prejudice is evident For only if we approach the world with a kind of invincible bias, that we should believe in accordance with what has been perceived in the past, can we discount all claims for the miraculous.

There are two important objections to this reasoning. First, Hume is inconsistent with his own epistemology. Hume himself recognizes the fallacy of this kind of reasoning when he argues that, based on past conformity, nothing can be known as true concerning the future. We cannot even know for sure that the sun will rise tomorrow morning. Hence, for Hume to deny future miracles based on past experience is inconsistent with his own principles and violates his own system.

Second, if it were true that no present exception can overthrow "laws" based on our uniform experience in the past, then there could be no true progress in our scientific understanding of the world. For established or repeatable exceptions to past patterns are precisely what force a change in scientific belief. When an observed exception to a past "law" is established, that "law" (L^1) is revised and a new "law" (L^2) replaces it. This is precisely what happened when certain outerspatial "exceptions" to Newton's law of gravitation were found and Einstein's theory of relativity was considered broader and more adequate. Without established exceptions, no progress can be made in science. In short, Hume's objections to miracles seem to be unscientific! Exceptions to "laws" have a heuristic value; they are goads to progress in our understanding of the universe.

Hume offers a forceful argument against miracles. But, strong as it may seem, he is overly optimistic to believe this argument can be "an everlasting check" and "useful as long as the world endures" to refute any credible claim for the miraculous. In point of fact, for several reasons Hume's argument is not successful. First, in the "hard" form he begs the question by assuming miracles are by definition impossible. Second, Hume is inconsistent with his own epistemology, and makes scientific progress impossible. In brief, to eliminate miracles before looking at them seems prejudicial, and not to do this is to leave the door open to their possibility. Wise persons do not legislate in advance that miracles cannot be believed to have happened; rather they look at the evidence to see if they did occur. For the rational mind, Hume's efforts to eliminate miracles must be considered unsuccessful.

 **3**

ARE MIRACLES IRRATIONAL?

> A rape [of the mind] is committed when individuals reporting
> extraordinary events, and in fact laying down their lives on
> behalf of their witness, are declared at the outset to be
> hotheaded enthusiasts, uncritical minds, or plain fakers. This is
> done on the patently dogmatic grounds that nature cannot
> change its course.—Stanley Jaki

As THE ARGUMENTS against miracles proceed, it becomes obvious that the matter is not simply a factual one; it is a philosophical one. Indeed, in the final analysis it is not simply a matter of thought but of choice. This choice has been expressed in "scientific" objections stated by British atheist Antony Flew.

Flew's Argument from Unrepeatability

Flew has been a lecturer in philosophy at three major British universities, including Oxford and Aberdeen. Later he became a professor of philosophy at the University of Keele. As a contemporary philosopher of the analytical school, Flew is well known in the philosophical world for his works in philosophical theology. He has authored and edited numerous books and articles in scholarly journals and has been especially recognized for his arguments against miracles.

The Statement of Flew's Argument

Flew argues against miracles on the grounds that they are unrepeatable. As he sees it, Hume's argument really amounts to something like this:

33

1. Every miracle is a violation of a law of nature.
2. The evidence against any violation of nature is the strongest possible evidence.
3. Therefore, the evidence against miracles is the strongest possible evidence.

Flew says that "Hume was primarily concerned, not with the question of fact, but with that of evidence. The problem was how the occurrence of a miracle could be proved, rather than whether any such events had ever occurred." However, adds Flew, "our sole ground for characterizing the reported occurrence as miraculous is at the same time a sufficient reason for calling it physically impossible." Why, we may ask, is this so? Because "the critical historian, confronted with some story of a miracle, will usually dismiss it out of hand."

On what grounds are miracles dismissed by the critical historian? "To justify his procedure he will have to appeal to precisely the principle which Hume advanced: the 'absolute impossibility or miraculous nature' of the events attested must, 'in the eyes of all reasonable people . . . alone be regarded as a sufficient refutation.'" In short, even though miracles are not logically impossible, they are scientifically impossible, "For it is only and precisely by presuming that the laws that hold today held in the past . . . that we can rationally interpret the detritus [fragments] of the past as evidence and from it construct our account of what actually happened."[1]

As to the charge that this uniformitarian approach to history is "irrationally dogmatic," Flew answers with what is really the heart of his amplification of Hume's argument. First, "as Hume was insisting from first to last, the possibility of miracles is a matter of evidence and not of dogmatism." Further, "the proposition reporting the (alleged) occurrence of the miracle will be singular, particular, and in the past tense." Propositions of this sort "cannot any longer be tested directly. It is this that gives propositions of the first sort [i.e., of the general and repeatable] the vastly greater logical strength."[2]

Flew's argument can be stated as follows:

1. Miracles are by nature particular and unrepeatable.
2. Natural events are by nature general and repeatable.
3. In practice, the evidence for the general and repeatable is always greater than that for the particular and unrepeatable.

1. Antony Flew, "Miracles," in *The Encyclopedia of Philosophy*, ed. Paul Edwards (New York: Macmillan, 1967), 5:351.
2. Ibid.

4. Therefore, in practice, the evidence will always be greater against miracles than for them.

For Flew generality and repeatability (in the present) are what give natural events greater evidential value than miracles. And since, of course, it will always be this way in the future, the evidence against miracles will always be greater than the evidence for them.

An Evaluation of Flew's Argument

There are several things that should be observed about Flew's argument. First, most modern naturalists, such as Flew, accept some irrepeatable singularities of their own. Many contemporary astronomers believe in the singular origin of the universe by a "Big Bang." And nearly all scientists believe that the origin of life on this planet is a singular event that has never been repeated here. But if Flew's argument against miracles is correct, then it is also wrong for scientists to believe in these singularities that many of them consider to be natural events. Thus Flew's argument against supernaturalism would also eliminate some basic naturalistic belief(s).

Second, Flew's view is subject to his own criticism of theists, namely, it is an unfalsifiable position. For no matter what state of affairs actually occurs (even a resurrection), Flew (contrary even to Hume's claims) would be obliged to believe it was not a miracle. For Flew argues that "it often seems to people who are not religious as if there was no conceivable event or series of events the occurrence of which would be admitted by sophisticated religious people to be a sufficient reason for conceding 'there wasn't a God after all.'" In short, their belief is in actuality unfalsifiable.

But in like manner we may ask Flew (rephrasing his own words), "What would have to occur or to have occurred to constitute for you a disproof of . . . your antisupernaturalism?"[3] Flew's answer is: No event in the world would falsify his naturalism, because in practice he believes the evidence is always greater against miracles than for them. Nor does it help for Flew to claim that his antisupernaturalism is falsifiable in principle but never in practice, on the grounds that in practice the evidence will always be greater for the repeatable. For surely he would then have to allow the theist to claim that, in principle, the existence of God is falsifiable but that, in practice, no

---

3. Antony Flew, "Theology and Falsification," in *The Existence of God*, ed. John Hick (New York: Macmillan, 1964), p. 227.

event could disconfirm God's existence! The fact that Flew and other nontheists attempt to disprove God by arguing from the fact of evil in the world reveals their belief that falsification in practice is that with which they are really concerned.

The truth is that we cannot have it both ways. If naturalism is unfalsifiable in practice, then belief in God (or in miracles) can also be unfalsifiable in practice. On the other hand, if supernaturalism can never be established in practice, then neither can naturalism be so established. For it is always possible for the theist to claim of every alleged "natural" event that God is the ultimate cause of it. The theist may insist that all natural events (i.e., naturally repeatable ones) are the way God normally operates and that "miraculous" events are the way God works on special occasions. Now, on Flew's own grounds, there is no way in practice to falsify this theistic belief. For, again, just as Flew claims that naturalism is unfalsifiable in practice, so too the theist could claim the same for theism. For no matter what events in the natural world are produced (repeatable or unrepeatable), the theist can still claim that God is the ultimate cause of it, and, on Flew's grounds, no naturalist can disprove this theistic claim.[4]

Third, we may object to Flew's assumption that the repeatable always evidentially outweighs the unrepeatable. If this were so, then as Richard Whately points out (see chap. 2), we could not believe in the historicity of any unusual events from the past (none of which are repeatable). In fact, if repeatability in practice is the true test of superior evidence, then we should not believe that observed births or deaths occurred, for birth and death are both unrepeatable in practice. Likewise, even historical geology is unrepeatable in practice, as is the history of our planet. Hence, if Flew were right, the science of geology should be eliminated too!

Scientists do not reject unrepeated singularities out of hand. "Luckily for science, scientists relatively rarely brush aside reports about a really new case with the remark: 'It cannot be really different from the thousand other cases we have already investigated.' The brave reply of the young assistant, 'But, Sir, what if this is the thousand and first case?'

4. It will not do for the naturalist to attempt a reductio ad absurdum and insist that God causes all natural events, and therefore causes evil. For this argument begs the question in assuming that God has no good purpose for these natural events. Further, the theist denies that God is the cause of evil (for which he has a good purpose); the immediate cause of evil is some free agent(s) God permits to operate for the ultimate good known to himself. For further discussion of this point, see Norman L. Geisler, *Roots of Evil* (Richardson, Tex.: Word, 1989).

which . . . is precisely the rejoinder that is to be offered in connection with facts that fall under suspicion because of their miraculous character."[5] So, if naturalists push their arguments far enough to eliminate miracles, by implication they thereby eliminate the grounds for their own beliefs. If they qualify them so as to include all the natural and scientific data they wish, then they reopen the door for miracles.

Chryssides' Argument Against Miracles

The Statement of Chryssides' Argument

George Chryssides, professor of philosophy at Plymouth Polytechnic in Plymouth, England, has expounded an objection to miracles based on the repeatability principle. We may summarize Chryssides' reasoning this way:

1. No event can be attributed to a rational agent unless its occurrence is regular and repeatable.
2. Miracles are by nature not regular or repeatable.
3. Therefore, no miracle can be attributed to any rational agent (e.g., to God).

Technically, Chryssides is raising the problem of the identifiability of miracles (which will be discussed in chap. 5), but since his argument is based on the unrepeatability of miracles, we will discuss this aspect here. The crucial premise in Chryssides' argument is the first one. It is based on the view that regularity or repeatability is the only way to know that a given event is caused by a rational agent. Chryssides writes, "My argument will be that, if the concept of a violation of scientific regularity makes sense . . . and even if . . . such a violation could be identified, it would be logically impossible to ascribe such an event to the activity of a rational agent."[6]

For example, argues Chryssides, "Suppose Jones sees a mountain in the distance and says to the mountain, 'Mountain, cast yourself into the sea!,' whereupon the mountain is observed to rise up from its surroundings and fall into the water." If this occurred, "why should we

5. Stanley Jaki, *Miracles and Physics* (Front Royal, Va.: Christendom, 1989), p. 100.
6. George D. Chryssides, "Miracles and Agents," *Religious Studies* 11 (Sept. 1975): 321.
7. Ibid., p. 319.
8. Ibid., p. 322.

say that Jones moved the mountain, rather than . . . by a strange coincidence the mountain happened to move . . . and fall into the water?"[7]

The crux of this argument is a premise (similar to the one offered by Hume) that a "necessary condition of the attribution of causality is . . . the Repeatability Requirement."[8] In short, a single instance cannot establish that there is a rational agent behind the event; it could simply be a "fluke." Only if we can perform the event on command over and over can we claim to be the rational cause of it.

Chryssides offers several qualifications of this repeatability principle. Repeatability does not imply: (1) that we can predict the time of the event; (2) that the given event must occur many times (as long as similar events have occurred); (3) that the agent is capable of repeating the event (e.g., a lucky croquet shot); (4) that the antecedent conditions of the event can be specified by anyone in practice, but only in principle; (5) that the constant conjunction must be absolute (as Hume implied), but only that it must be regular; (6) that repeatability is a sufficient condition (since we could command a grandfather's clock to chime every hour without being the cause of the chiming).

Further, insists Chryssides, we must define an event in "such a way that its repetition is not logically impossible." What is necessary is to assert that "similar events will follow similar actions of human agents."[9] Or, to return to the example of Jones' "apparently moving the mountain, we may say that agency can be ascribed to Jones only if repetition of similar putative causes is accompanied by a repetition of similar putative effects. But if there is such regularity, this is statable in terms of scientific law, and if there is not, then agency cannot be ascribed."[10] In short, "a 'miracle' in this sense is logically impossible." For "the believer in miracles seems to wish to claim that the events he so describes are both caused and uncaused at the same time; they are caused, he says, in that they are due to the activity of an agent; they are uncaused, he says, in that they cannot be subsumed under scientific regularity. But he cannot have it both ways."[11]

An Evaluation of Chryssides' Argument

Several points may be made in reply to Chryssides. First, his demands for determining if an event has a rational cause are too nar-

9. Ibid., p. 325.
10. Ibid., p. 326.
11. Ibid., p. 327.

row. Repeatability is not the only way to determine rationality. It can be determined by examining the nature of the effect. For example, by looking at one great work of art, we can know it had an intelligent cause. This is true even if we or anyone else we know cannot repeat the feat in practice. Furthermore, an event may be repeatable in principle, even though it is not actually repeated in practice. Not every song Handel wrote was a "Hallelujah Chorus," but would we deny that this song was a result of rational agency, even if we know nothing about the composer? This unique work bears the unmistakable mark of intelligent authorship.

Second, regularity is not the only (or even the best) sign of rational agency; so is specified complexity such as is found in a human language or in the genetic code.[12] All we need to hear is a single clear SOS signal over a ship radio during a storm to know that it was sent by a rational agent. Such a brief but intelligible message in that context is enough to indicate an intelligent cause. Likewise, most scientists who are listening for radio signals from outer space would accept the reception of only one or, at most, a few intelligible messages, as proof of extraterrestrial intelligent existence. In truth, repeatability is not as good an indication of rational agency as is intelligibility. Any scientist who saw even one message in alphabet cereal spilled on the breakfast table reading "Take out the garbage. Love, Mary" would not hesitate to conclude an intelligent being had formed the words. It would not have to be repeated every morning for days or weeks before the scientist came to that conclusion.

This leads to a third objection to Chryssides' view. Whether or not we attribute an event to a rational agent depends on the context. For instance, if we see the three letters SOS in the middle of alphabet soup, we probably will not assume that a ship is in distress; whereas the same letters on a ship radio in a storm would be a sign of an intelligent agent. Likewise, fire from the sky consuming an animal on an altar is not, as such, a proof that God did it. In the context of a theistic world and a prophet calling on God to vindicate the true God over false gods, however, it is a different matter (see 1 Kings 18)! The crux of the matter as to whether God is the cause of an event will depend on the total theistic-moral context of the event (see chap. 9).

12. See Norman L. Geisler and Kerby Anderson, *Origin Science* (Grand Rapids: Baker, 1988), chap. 7.
13. Ibid., p. 325.

Fourth, Chryssides is inconsistent. He argues that a "miracle" is logically impossible and yet insists that a natural event has repeatability and must be defined in "such a way that its repetition is not logically impossible."[13] How can he rule out supernaturalism logically and yet insist that naturalism cannot be eliminated in the same way? But if the rules of the game are "heads the naturalist wins, and tails the supernaturalist loses," then there is not much chance for a rational belief in miracles.

Fifth, Chryssides' position dies a death by qualification. By the time he finishes qualifying what repeatability means, the supernaturalist can claim similar theistic conditions for miracles. Chryssides admits that the event need not be predictable in advance, repeated more than once, or have to specify its conditions in advance. But by the same logic his objections against miracles lose most of their force too. Further, we can be more sure of the intelligent cause of some things that happened only once (e.g., the faces on Mount Rushmore), than we can of the specific cause of some things that occur regularly (e.g., what holds the atom together).

The only real difference Chryssides can point to is one readily granted by the theist, namely, that natural events can occur more often than miracles. But, as we have seen, this difference is not crucial to determining rational agency. Furthermore, if miracles occurred often enough to determine that they are not pure flukes and can be repeated, then even this criterion can be met. And the Bible records hundreds of them. The real question is not how regularly a "miracle" must occur to count as an act of God (Chryssides admits that many actual occurrences are unnecessary), but whether any miracles do indeed occur. And this possibility cannot be eliminated by philosophy (unless we can disprove the existence of God); rather, it is a matter of history (see chap. 12).

Both Flew and Chryssides develop Hume's principle of "constant conjunction" into a repeatability criterion for eliminating the miraculous (or at least a credible knowledge of it). Both, however, fail because they either beg the question by assuming naturalism is true, or else destroy their position by qualification. In brief, if we take a narrow definition of natural law, then, along with miracles, we eliminate some natural event as well. And if we qualify and broaden our definition of natural law, then we make room for miracles too.

The fact that naturalists have found it necessary to change the definition of the natural indicates that their reasons for trying to eliminate miracles are not strictly scientific. Once, in a very revealing admission, an Ivy League physics professor told me that his "reason" for accepting a naturalistic perspective was that "it is ethically more comfortable to believe this way." In fact, Julian Huxley admitted that he received a great sense of relief in believing that God does not exist. This, then, is not a matter of scientific fact but of moral choice.

The attempts to eliminate miracles have become increasingly less rational and more a matter of faith. Spinoza argued that miracles were impossible. Hume said they were incredible. But, if correct, our analysis has shown that it is basically a matter of belief. Indeed, in many respects (as the critique of Flew reveals) the disbelief in miracles is often actually unfalsifiable.

The difference between how Hume and Chryssides handle the question of whether specific events would be miracles illustrates our point. Hume believes that if someone walks on water it is miraculous, but Chryssides denies this. The believer in the miraculous is tempted to ask, if walking on water, moving mountains on command, and raising the dead do not qualify as miracles, then what does? It would seem that the naturalists are changing the rules in order to explain away miracles that they cannot easily deny have happened.

This point is forcefully made in the story of the psychotic patient who thought he was dead. Seemingly no empirical test could convince him that he was alive. He would claim that dead people can feel and see. Finally, in desperation, the doctor asked him if dead men could bleed. "No," he replied. "Aha," said the doctor, who promptly punctured the patient's finger with a pin. Seeing the blood, the patient cried, "My goodness, dead people do bleed!"

4

ARE MIRACLES UNSCIENTIFIC?

> It is not contrary to the laws of Nature. . . . The laws of
> Nature are never broken. Your mistake is to think that the
> little regularities we have observed on our planet for a few
> hundred years are the real unbreakable laws; whereas they are
> only the remote results which the true laws bring about more
> often than not.—C. S. Lewis

MODERN LIFE IS LARGELY a product of the scientific method. Automobiles, radios, televisions, jets, space exploration, satellites, and computers are all part of our way of life. Few people are willing to leave all that our scientific civilization has provided and head for the jungle. It is for this reason that many are rejecting miracles. For they insist that the acceptance of the scientific method means the rejection of miracles. In the wake of modern science it has been common for naturalists to attach their position to the scientific method. The result is that belief in miracles is held to be contrary to the scientific method. In short, miracles are held to be unscientific.

Miracles Are Contrary to Scientific Explanation

The Nowell-Smith Position

Patrick Nowell-Smith, professor of philosophy at York University in Toronto, objects to the supernaturalist's claim that an event is a miracle simply because it cannot be explained in terms of scientific laws. He writes, "We may believe him [the supernaturalist] when he says that no scientific method or hypothesis known to him will

43

explain it." But "to say that it is inexplicable as a result of natural agents is already beyond his competence as a scientist, and to say that it must be ascribed to supernatural agents is to say something that no one could possibly have the right to affirm on the evidence alone."[1]

Nowell-Smith argues that "no matter how strange an event someone reports, the statement that it must have been due to a supernatural agent cannot be a part of that report."[2] The reason for this rejection is clear. From the fact "that no scientist can at present explain certain phenomena," says Nowell-Smith, "it does not follow that the phenomena are inexplicable by scientific methods, still less that they must be attributed to supernatural agents."[3] That is, "there is still the possibility that science may be able, in the future, to offer an explanation which, though couched in quite new terms, remains strictly scientific."[4]

Nowell-Smith's argument can be summarized as follows:

1. The scientifically unexplained is not necessarily the scientifically unexplainable.
2. "Miracles" are scientifically unexplained.
3. Therefore "miracles" are not necessarily scientifically unexplainable.

A good example of this is the fact that for many years it was held that bumblebee flight was unexplainable by natural law. The principles of this very natural occurrence, however, have come to light in the discovery of power packs in the mitochondria, which make rapid wing motion possible. This illustrates the folly of insisting that a presently unexplained event must be due to supernatural agents.

What is a scientific type of explanation? According to Nowell-Smith, "a scientific explanation is an hypothesis from which predictions can be made, which can afterwards be verified."[5] In addition, "an explanation must explain how an event comes about; otherwise it is simply a learned . . . name for the phenomenon to be explained." In view of this definition, "if miracles are 'lawful' it

1. Patrick Nowell-Smith, "Miracles," in *New Essays in Philosophical Theology*, eds. Antony Flew and Alisdair MacIntyre (New York: Macmillan, 1955), pp. 245–46.
2. Ibid., p. 246.
3. Ibid., p. 247.
4. Ibid., p. 248.
5. Ibid., p. 249.

should be possible to state the laws; if not, the alleged explanation amounts to a confession that they are explicable." For "if we can detect any order in God's interventions it should be possible to extrapolate in the usual way and to predict when and how a miracle will occur . . . otherwise the hypothesis is not either to confirmation or refutation."[6]

Nowell-Smith concludes with this challenge to the supernaturalist: "Let him consider the meaning of the word 'explanation' and let him ask himself whether this notion does not involve that of a law or hypothesis capable of predictive expansion. And then let him ask himself whether such an explanation would not be natural, in whatever terms it was couched, and how the notion of 'the supernatural' could play any part in it."[7] Should the supernaturalist object that he is simply redefining the "natural" to include miracles, Nowell-Smith replies: "I do not wish to quarrel about words. I will concede your supernatural, if this is all that it means. For the supernatural will be nothing but a new field for scientific inquiry, a field as different from physics as physics is from psychology, but not differing in principle or requiring any non-scientific method."[8]

We may now summarize the foregoing argument:

1. Only what has predictive capabilities can qualify as an explanation of an event.
2. A miracle explanation cannot make verifiable predictions.
3. Therefore, a miracle explanation does not qualify as an explanation of any event.

The long and short of this is that only scientific explanations can qualify as explanations, since only scientific explanations have predictive abilities. Hence, either miracles become scientific explanations or cease being explanations altogether. In brief, a miracle is methodologically unscientific. It is contrary to the scientific means of explaining events, a way that always involves the ability to predict similar events.

Further, Nowell-Smith denies that rational agency is necessary to account for any anomaly of nature. Such aberrations will in time yield to application of scientific method. All that happens will eventually be shown to result from natural law.

6. Ibid., p. 251.
7. Ibid., p. 253.
8. Ibid.

An Evaluation of Nowell-Smith's Antisupernaturalism

Despite the fact that he claims "the problem must be attacked with an open mind, that is to say, with a mind not disposed to reject evidence because it conflicts with some preconceived theory,"[9] Nowell-Smith evidences an invincible bias in favor of naturalism. For, in practice, any event in the world will ipso facto be declared by him to be a natural event. But if no event is ever permitted to have a miraculous interpretation, how can this be considered an "open-minded" view? He is in fact only open to naturalistic interpretations.

That Nowell-Smith is really begging the question in favor of naturalism is evident for several reasons. First, he defines "explanation" in such a narrow way as to eliminate the possibility of a supernatural explanation. Rather than being truly open to another kind of explanation than a natural one, he arbitrarily insists that all explanations must be naturalistic ones or else they do not really count as explanations.

The supernaturalist does not insist that "an event no matter how strange must have been due to a supernatural agent." It does seem likely that most strange events are natural, although as yet unaccounted for. But the supernaturalist does object to Nowell-Smith's saying that supernatural agency "cannot" ever be part of the report of a strange event. The supernaturalist says that we should look at the alleged event to see if it was or was not a miracle. What the supernaturalist objects to is the naturalist's dogmatic assertion, before even considering the evidence, that no miracle occurred.

Second, Nowell-Smith simply assumes without proof that "all phenomena will *ultimately* admit of a natural explanation."[10] But how does he know this is so? Not as a scientist. For there is no empirical proof for this assumption. It is simply a matter of naturalistic faith!

Third, even if he were presented with empirical evidence of a miracle, Nowell-Smith makes it very clear that he would never admit that it is really a supernatural event. He will simply hope that some day, "ultimately," someone will find a naturalistic explanation. Meanwhile, he will persist in believing that such an explanation can be found.

Fourth, Nowell-Smith demands that all explanations have predictive value to qualify as true explanations. And yet there are many events he would call natural that no one can predict. We cannot predict if or when a bachelor will marry. But when he does say, "I do,"

9. Ibid., p. 243.
10. Ibid., p. 247, emphasis added.

do we not claim that he was simply "doing what comes naturally"? If naturalists reply, as indeed they must, that they cannot always predict in practice (but only in principle) when natural events will occur, then supernaturalists can do likewise. In principle we know that a miracle will occur whenever God deems one necessary. If we knew all the facts (which include the mind of God), then we could predict in practice precisely when this would be.

Furthermore, biblical miracles are past singularities that, like the origin of the universe or of life, are not presently being repeated. But predictions cannot be made from singularities. They can only be projected from patterns. The past is not known by empirical science, but by a forensic science. Therefore, it is misdirected to ask for predictions (forward); rather, one is attempting to make a retrodiction (backward).

Fifth, Nowell-Smith shows the extent he is willing to go to exclude miracles as an explanation of some strange event. He begins by insisting that "the breakdown of *all* explanations in terms of present-day science does not . . . immediately force us outside the realm of the 'natural.'"[11] The supernaturalist can (and does) agree with Nowell-Smith who admits "that the present hypotheses of science can never be expanded to cover miraculous phenomena." But the supernaturalist parts company with Nowell-Smith when he insists that "we may require new concepts and new laws."[12] This insistence on ultimate natural causes for miracles is the essence of the naturalist mindset. Such a position goes beyond what is warranted by the evidence. At this juncture, the naturalist demonstrates a faith commitment that rivals the religious dedication of the most ardent miracle-believers.

Sixth, one of the problems behind this kind of scientific naturalism is the confusion of naturalistic *origin* and natural *function*. Motors function in accordance with physical laws but physical laws do not produce motors; minds do. In like manner, the origin of a miracle is not the physical and chemical laws of the universe, even though the resulting event will operate in accordance with these natural laws. In other words, a miraculous conception will produce a nine-month pregnancy (in accordance with natural law). So, while natural laws regulate the operation of things, they do not account for the origin of all things.

11. Ibid., p. 248, emphasis added.
12. Ibid., p. 251.

Miracles Are Contrary to the Scientific Method

While Nowell-Smith pronounces miracles unscientific by virtue of their being contrary to scientific *explanation*, others have argued that miracles are contrary to the scientific *method*.

Miracles Are Contrary to Science as Science

One proponent of this view, Alastair McKinnon, puts the argument this way:

1. A scientific law is a generalization based on past observation.
2. Any exception to a scientific law invalidates that law as such and calls for a revision of it.
3. A miracle is an exception to a scientific law.
4. Therefore, any so-called miracle would call for a revision of the present scientific law.

That is, a miracle would be assumed to be a natural event under a new law that incorporates it into its natural explanation. This means laws are like maps, and maps are never violated; they are only revised when they are found to be incorrect.

Even naturalists have admitted that this argument is easily refuted. As one put it, "This a priori argument can be refuted by noting that a supernaturally caused exception to a scientific law would not invalidate it, because scientific laws are designed to express regularities"; in the case of a miracle we have "a special and non-repeatable" exception.[13] That is to say, one nonrepeatable exception does not call for the revision of a natural law. More likely it would be credited to faulty observation. From a strictly scientific point of view a nonrepeatable exception remains just that—an exception to known scientific laws. If, under specified conditions, the anomaly recurs, then and only then does a scientist have the right to call it a natural event. In this case, anomalies would be pointers to the development of a more general natural law.

Miracles, however, are not the result of natural laws. They are occurrences that were caused to happen by the willful actions of rational agents (God or his representatives). That action of will is what cannot be repeated and therefore places miracles outside the realm of scientific observation. In other words, when a miracle takes place, it is because God wants it to. We cannot arrange for God to

13. Malcolm L. Diamond, "Miracles," *Religious Studies* 9 (Sept. 1973): 316–17.

"want to" cause one again simply so that we can watch. Miracles do not change our view of scientific laws, as progress in science does; miracles simply step outside of those laws.

As has been observed, scientists and philosophers are really interested only in *repeatable* exceptions to known laws. Miracles leave natural laws intact and therefore are not unscientific: "Miracles are not experimental, repeatable. They are particular, peculiar events. . . . They are not small-scale laws. Consequently they do not destroy large-scale laws; . . . they have not the genuine deadly power of the negative instance."[14]

Diamond's Argument That Miracles Would Destroy Science

Malcolm Diamond, professor of philosophy at Princeton University, insists that it is disastrous to accept miraculous exceptions to scientific laws. For if we accept some exceptions as supernatural, then "scientific development would either be stopped or else made completely capricious, because it would necessarily be a matter of whim or whether one invoked the concept of miracle."[15] In short, Diamond sees two problems with supernaturalism: (1) exceptions should not stop scientific research (they are in fact goads to further research); and (2) exceptions should not necessarily be called miracles. Does the odd always prove God? If not, then how do we distinguish the unusual from the supernatural?

According to Diamond, "Allowing for the possibility of supernatural explanations of naturally observable occurrences is something that would, in effect, drive working scientists to opt right out of the scientific enterprise." Why? "Because," insists Diamond, "these scientists would not be able to investigate [the miracle]. . . . As scientists they would not be able to determine whether the exception was supernatural."[16] In short, "scientists, as scientists, must operate with autonomy, that is, they must set their own rules and referee their own games. Therefore, although nothing logically would prevent a scientist from accepting the supernatural interpretation of an utterly extraordinary occurrence, on the functional level, this would involve a sellout of science."[17]

Diamond concludes: "the answer that I shall offer on behalf of the naturalistic interpretation is pragmatic. It recommends reliance

14. Ninian Smart, *Philosophers and Religious Truth* (London: SCM, 1964), p. 41.
15. Guy Robinson, quoted in Diamond, "Miracles," p. 317.
16. Ibid., p. 320.
17. Ibid., p. 321.

on the scientific explanations without pretending to be a conclusive refutation of supernaturalism."[18]

The outline of this argument is now clear. It is a pragmatic argument based on belief in the autonomy of the scientific method, which can be formulated thus:

1. Scientists, as scientists, cannot give up looking for naturalistic explanations for every event.
2. To admit even one miracle is to give up looking for a natural explanation.
3. Therefore, to admit miracles is to give up being a scientist.

An Evaluation of Diamond's Charge

We are now in a position to evaluate the charge that belief in miracles is unscientific. Diamond's comments make evident his basic assumption of the absolute autonomy of the scientific method. He assumes as a matter of faith (with only pragmatic justification) that the scientific method is *the* method for determining all truth. Indeed, it is not just the scientific method but one aspect of the scientific approach (namely, the search for natural causes) that is assumed to be the only approach to truth. The following criticisms, then, may be offered against Diamond's arguments.

First, it is wrong, as Diamond implies, to presuppose that the scientific method necessarily entails naturalism. Scientists as scientists need not be so narrow as to believe, in advance of looking at every event, that nothing can ever count as a miracle. All a scientist needs to hold is premises like "every event has a cause" and "the observable universe operates in an orderly way." To add that "every event has a *natural* cause" is to load the scientific method with naturalistic presuppositions.

Second, Diamond strongly assumes that science has dominion over every event when, in fact, the proper domain of operation science is only over *regular* events. To assume that there is a natural explanation for every irregular, unrepeatable event is not science but metaphysics. Natural laws do not account for the origin of all events any more than the laws of physics alone explain the origin of a motor, or than the laws of grammar alone can account for a poem.

18. Ibid. For more on the relationship between science and theology, see J. P. Moreland, *Christianity and the Nature of Science* (Grand Rapids: Baker, 1989).

Natural laws only account for the operation of these things, not their origin. It takes an intelligent cause to explain their origin.

Third, it is not scientific to be closed-minded to reasonable explanations. And if there is a God who caused the universe to exist and who cares for it, then it is not unreasonable to expect that he can perform some regular activities (natural "laws") and also some special events ("miracles"). The only way to effectively disprove this possibility is to disprove that God exists, but most atheists agree that this is, strictly speaking, not possible to do.[19] Conversely, if God exists, then miracles are possible. The truly scientific and open-minded person will not dismiss in advance, logically or methodologically, the possibility of identifying some miraculous events. We must not presuppose, as Diamond does, that "scientists, as scientists, must operate with [naturalistic] autonomy."[20]

Fourth, when we reduce the argument against miracles to its basic premises it amounts to this:

1. Whatever actually occurs in the natural world is a natural event.
2. Some so-called miracles have actually occurred.
3. Therefore, these so-called miracles are really natural events.

Now the circular nature of the naturalist's argument is laid bare. Whatever happens in the natural world is, ipso facto, a natural event! The fallacy is obvious: whatever occurs *in* nature was caused *by* nature. Even Michael Polanyi seems to fall into this trap when he writes, "if the conversion of water into wine or the resurrection of the dead could be experimentally verified, this would strictly disprove their miraculous nature. Indeed, to the extent to which any event can be established in terms of natural science, it belongs to the natural order of things."[21] This, of course, assumes what is to be proven, namely, that there is no supernatural being (God) who can act in nature. Just because an event occurs in the world does not mean it was caused by the world. It may have been specially caused by the God who exists beyond the world.

19. See Norman L. Geisler, *Christian Apologetics* (Grand Rapids: Baker, 1976), chap. 12, for further discussion of this point.
20. Diamond, "Miracles," p. 321.
21. Cited by Stanley Jaki, *Miracles and Physics* (Front Royal, Va.: Christendom, 1989), p. 78.

The Integrity of the Scientific Method

If miracles are allowed, how can we retain the integrity of the scientific method? If some events are ruled out of bounds to scientists, then has not the supernaturalist closed the door to rational examination of some events? Or, even more to the point, once we allow miracles, how can there be a meaningfully definable role for scientific exploration?

Two things should be noted in response. First, positing a supernatural cause for the origin of some rare events in no way affects the domain of science. Science is based on a regular pattern of events, not on rare ones. The scientific method, therefore, has every right to demand explanatory control over all regular events. But science as such has no right to claim that it alone can provide a scientific explanation for all singularities.

Second, science has unlimited authority in the classification of regular events, but it is not unlimited in the naturalistic explanation of singular events. That is, scientists have a right—even an obligation—to examine all events, including anomalies. If they cannot specify how a singular, unrepeated event is part of a regular pattern, however, then as scientists, they must place some events in the class of "not yet explainable as natural events." Of these, some may have a supernatural cause, but simply to assume that all "not yet explained" events must thereby be naturally explainable goes beyond science as such. It moves into a philosophical belief in naturalism. Until scientists can show that this event is part of a regular, repeatable pattern, their classification of it as a naturally caused event is not a matter of science, but of naturalistic faith.

Various attempts have been made by naturalists to prove that miracles are unscientific. Some have insisted that believing in miracles is contrary to scientific explanations; others say it is contrary to scientific methodology. The first group argues that miracles, contrary to natural laws, are unpredictable; others contend that miracles are unrepeatable or would sacrifice the autonomy of science. In each case, it has been shown that the arguments beg the question in favor of naturalism. That is, they assume the scientific method must be defined in such a way as to exclude the acceptance of miracles. In effect, they have insisted that, by its very nature, the scientific method dictates in advance that every event must be considered natural. The central but hidden premise is invincibly antisupernatural:

"Every event in the world must be assumed to be a naturally caused event." If we do not now have a naturalistic explanation, then we must never give up believing that "ultimately" there is one. Of course, supernaturalists cry, "Unfair!" They point out that we do not have to be incorrigibly naturalistic to be scientific. Properly speaking, the domain of scientific law is only the realm of regular events, not all events.

Contrary to the views of Nowell-Smith, miracles do not destroy the integrity of the scientific method. Science is possible as long as we assume, as theists do, that the world is orderly and regular and that it operates in accordance with the law of causality. In point of fact, some noted modern philosophers such as Alfred North Whitehead have observed that Christianity is really the mother of science.[22] Philosopher-scientist Ian Barbour claims that it was specifically the Christian belief in creation that provided much of the impetus for modern science.[23] But if the origin of the world can have a supernatural cause without violating the laws by which it operates, then God can be the cause of other events in the world (miracles) without violating the regular way nature operates. Since empirical science deals only with the way things operate, not the way they originate, the origination of an event by a supernatural cause (e.g., a miracle) in no way violates any natural law.

Furthermore, simply because most events are regular and naturally predictable does not mean that all events are. Nor does the fact that every event has a cause mean that every cause must be a natural one. The fact that science should be allowed a rational examination (and classification) of all regular events does not mean that it must give a naturalistic explanation for all events, including unrepeated singularities. If the evidence does not support a natural explanation of a singularity, then the scientific approach should not rule out the possibility of a miracle.

22. Alfred North Whitehead, *Science and the Modern World* (orig. 1925; New York: Free, 1967), chaps. 1, 11.
23. Ian Barbour, *Issues in Science and Religion* (Englewood Cliffs, N.J.: Prentice-Hall, 1966).

 **5**

ARE MIRACLES IDENTIFIABLE?

> But those men of science would in vain wait for an invitation
> from on High or from one of the Almighty's saintly agents.
> Miracles are not for order. They never were.—Stanley Jaki

SOME CONTEMPORARY NATURALISTS argue that no matter how
unusual an event is it cannot be identified as a miracle. If this argument is valid, it has serious implications for those who believe in miracles. First, it would mean that no unusual event that lays claim to a
divine origin could be considered a miracle. Further, theistic religions like Judaism and Christianity, in which miraculous claims are
central, could not actually identify any of their unusual events as miracles, no matter how much evidence they could produce for the
authenticity of these events.

There are two aspects to the case for the identifiability of miracles. First, miracles in general must be identifiable before a particular
miracle can be identified. Second, certain distinguishing marks
should serve to identify a specific event as a miracle.

Alastair McKinnon's Argument Against Miracles

According to some, miracles cannot be identified because the
concept of a miracle is not coherent. Alastair McKinnon claims that
"the idea of a suspension of natural law is self-contradictory. This
follows from the meaning of the term."[1] For if natural laws are
descriptive, as we argued in chapter 1, then they merely inform us

1. Cited in Richard Swinburne, *Miracles* (New York: Macmillan, 1989), p. 49.

55

about the actual course of events. But nothing, says McKinnon, can violate the actual course of events. "This contradiction may stand out more clearly if for natural law we substitute the expression the actual course of events. Miracle would then be defined as 'an event involving the suspension of the actual course of events.'" Therefore, "someone who insisted upon describing an event as a miracle would be in a rather odd position of claiming that its occurrence was contrary to the actual course of events."[2]

McKinnon's argument can be summarized as follows:

1. Natural laws describe the actual course of events.
2. A miracle is a violation of a natural law.
3. But it is impossible to violate the actual course of events (what is, is; what happens, happens).
4. Therefore, miracles are impossible.

Of course, if this is true, then miracles cannot be identified in the natural world, since whatever happens will not be a miracle. But herein lies the first and most basic problem with this argument. For if whatever happens is ipso facto a natural event, then of course miracles never happen. This, however, simply begs the question. This definition of natural law is loaded against miracles. For no matter what happens, it will automatically be called a natural event. That is, whatever happens within the natural world is a natural event. If so, this would eliminate in advance (by definition) the possibility of any event in the world ever being a miracle. But this fails to recognize even the possibility that not every event *in* the world is *of* the world. For a miracle can be an effect in nature by a cause that is beyond nature. For the mind that makes a computer is beyond the computer, and yet the computer that mind made is in the world.

This leads to the second point, namely, that McKinnon has misdefined natural laws. Natural laws should not be defined as what *actually* happens but what *regularly* happens. As Richard Swinburne points out, "laws of nature do not just describe what happens. . . . They describe what happens in a regular and predictable way." Therefore, "when what happens is entirely irregular and unpredictable, its occurrence is not something describable by natural laws."[3] Miracles, then, can be identified as events within nature that

2. Ibid., p. 50.
3. Ibid., p. 78.

fall into the class of the irregular and unpredictable. There may be more to a miracle than an irregular and unpredictable event in the natural world (see chap. 11), but they are not less than this. At any rate they cannot be ruled out simply by defining a natural law as what actually occurs. Even though they occur in the natural world miracles are distinguishable from naturally caused events.

Third, since natural laws deal with regularities and miracles with singularities, miracles cannot possibly be violations of natural laws. They are not even in the same class of events. A miracle is not a mini-natural law; it is a unique kind of event that has its own identifying characteristics (see chap. 9). Therefore, to claim that miracles do not happen (or should not be believed to have happened), because they do not fall into the class of natural events is a category mistake. By the same logic we might as well say that no book has an intelligent cause because its origin cannot be explained by the operational laws of physics and chemistry.

Another Objection to Identifying Miracles

Some philosophers object to miracles because miracles are regarded as contrary to the very nature of the scientific procedure for handling irregular or exceptional events. When scientists come upon an irregular or anomalous event they do not posit a miracle but simply revise their view and posit a broader natural law that includes this event. To do otherwise would be to forsake the scientific method. It would be to place "No Trespassing" signs on certain events in the natural world. But any event in the natural world is fair game for science. Nothing in nature can be considered out of bounds for scientific exploration. If it were, it would stultify scientific research. But a belief that certain events are miraculous would bar further scientific exploration. Hence, acceptance of miracles violates the proper domain of science.[4]

The argument can be summarized this way:

1. A miracle is an exception to a natural law.
2. In science exceptions are goals to a better explanation, not an indication to stop research.
3. Hence, acceptance of miracles would stop scientific research and progress.

4. See Ninian Smart, "Miracles and David Hume," in *Philosophers and Religious Truth* (London: SCM, 1964), chap. 2.

So a miracle could never be identified as an irregular event or anomaly, since for a scientist an anomaly does not cry "miracle." Rather, it calls for further research. When one natural law (L^1) does not explain this apparent exception, then scientists seek another natural law (L^2) that is broader and will include it. They do not throw in the towel and stop scientific research simply because the present law (explanation) is not broad enough to include this newly discovered exception to a previously held way of describing the situation. If this is the case, then a miracle cannot be identified as an exception to a regular pattern of events. For what is an exception to one scientific description (L^1) can be included within a broader description (L^2).

In response to this objection, two important things should be noted. First, like the previous objection it begs the question by insisting that every event is by its very nature a natural event. For if whatever happens—no matter how rare and unrepeatable—must not be considered a miracle, then miracles have been eliminated in advance by definition. It amounts to arguing that no event can be a miracle. Even if a resurrection from the dead occurred it could not be a miracle. In short, it is a form of methodological naturalism. For the very method it chooses to use does not admit the possibility of any event ever being identified as a miracle.

Furthermore, as some theists have pointed out, there is nothing in the scientific method that demands that *all* exceptional events be naturally caused but only that *repeatable* exceptions be so caused. If an exception to one scientific description (L^1) is not repeatable, then scientists have no right to posit a new law (L^2). For unless it is a repeatable event science has no right to claim it is a natural event. Nonrepeatable exceptions to known laws do not change those laws; they leave them intact. So there is no violation of a scientist's right to do science. Any regular, repeatable event is fair game for science. But since scientific laws are based on the *regular* and *repeatable*, scientists as scientists have no right to insist that every *irregular* and *nonrepeatable* event is also a natural event. To do so goes beyond science and reveals a naturalistic bias against miracles. In effect it erects its own "No Trespassing" sign on the world, one that demands "No Deity Allowed Here." But as theists have long insisted, if there is a God, then he cannot be locked out of his creation. For if he had the ability to create the universe to begin with (the ultimate exceptional act), then he certainly has the power to produce occasional but naturally unrepeatable exceptional acts within his world.

Thus the only effective way to disprove miracles is to disprove God. Certainly they cannot be rejected because all exceptional events belong to science. For unless an exception to a known scientific law (L^1) can be repeated there is no basis for positing another broader law (L^2) to explain it. Nonrepeatable exceptions (such as miracles are) do not come under the domain of natural laws.

Flew's Argument Against the Identifiability of Miracles

The basic objection to miracles by contemporary naturalists is not ontological but epistemological. That is, miracles are not rejected because they are known not to have occurred, but because they are not (or cannot be) known to have occurred. Flew's objection fits into this category.

Flew begins his discussion with this definition of a miracle: "A miracle is something which would never have happened had nature, as it were, been left to its own devices."[5] He notes that the great Christian theist Thomas Aquinas demonstrated that miracles are not properly a violation of natural law. Aquinas noted that "it is not against the principle of craftsmanship . . . if a craftsman effects a change in his product, even after he has given it its first form."[6] Not only is this power inherent in the idea of craftsmanship, so is the mind of the craftsman. So too a miracle bears the unmistakable mark not only of power but of divine mind. A miracle, then, is "a striking interposition of divine power by which the operations of the ordinary course of nature are overruled, suspended, or modified."[7]

Accepting this theistic definition of miracles, Flew goes on to insist that "exceptions are logic dependent upon rules. Only insofar as it can be shown that there is an order does it begin to be possible to show that the order is occasionally overridden."[8] In brief, miracles to Flew are logically parasitical to natural law. Hence, a strong view of miracles is possible without a strong view of the regularity of nature.

Flew quotes historian R. M. Grant to the effect that "credulity in antiquity varied inversely with the health of science and directly with the vigor of religion."[9] In short, miracles are prima facie improbable.

5. Antony Flew, "Miracles," in *The Encyclopedia of Philosophy*, ed. Paul Edwards (New York: Macmillan, 1967), 5:346.
6. Thomas Aquinas, *Summa contra Gentiles* 3.100.
7. Eric Mascall, quoted in Flew, "Miracles," p. 346.
8. Ibid., p. 347.
9. Ibid.

David Strauss, a nineteenth-century biblical critic, is even more skeptical: "We may summarily reject all miracles, prophecies, narratives of angels and demons, and the like, as simply impossible and irreconcilable with the known and universal laws which govern the course of events."[10] According to Flew, such skepticism is justified on a methodological basis.

Flew claims to be willing to allow (in principle at least) for the possibility of miracles (see chap. 3). In actual practice, however, he argues that there is a serious, if not insurmountable, problem—the problem of identifying a miracle.

The First Statement of Flew's Argument

The argument against miracles from their unidentifiability may be summarized as follows:

1. A miracle must be identifiable (distinguishable) before it can be known to have occurred.
2. There are only two ways to identify (distinguish) a miracle: in terms of nature or in terms of the supernatural.
3. But to identify it by reference to the supernatural (as an act of God) begs the question.
4. And to identify it in reference to the natural event robs it of its supernaturalness.
5. Therefore, miracles cannot be known to have occurred, since there is no way to identify them.

Flew insists, against Augustine,[11] that if a miracle is merely "a portent [which] is not contrary to nature, but contrary to our knowledge of nature,"[12] then it has no real apologetic value. For, argues Flew, if a miracle is merely a relativistic event to us at present, then it provides no proof that a revelation it alleges to support is really true. That is to say, whereas Augustine's notion of a miracle would assure the dependence of creation on God, it would do so only at the cost of subverting the apologetic value of a miracle.[13] For if a miracle is not really beyond the power of nature, but only contrary to our knowledge of nature, then a miracle is after all nothing but a natural

10. Quoted in ibid., p. 347.
11. Augustine, *City of God* 21.8.
12. Flew, "Miracles," p. 348.
13. Ibid.

event. In any event, we could not know that a miracle has really occurred, only that it *seems* to us that one did.

Flew's point can be stated another way. In order to identify a miracle within nature, the identification of that miracle must be in terms of what is independent of nature. But there is no way to identify a miracle as independent of the natural except by appealing to a supernatural realm, which begs the question. It argues in effect: "I know this is a miraculous event in the natural world, because I know (on some independent basis) that there is a supernatural cause beyond the natural world."

On the other hand, there is no natural way to identify a miracle. For unless it is already known (on independent grounds) that the event is miraculous, then it must be considered to be another natural event. From the scientific point of view, it is just "odd" or inconsistent with previously known events. Such an event should not occasion worship but should simply stimulate research for a broader scientific law that could include it.

From this Flew argues that it would follow that no alleged miraculous event can be used to prove that a religious system is true. That is to say, miracles can have no apologetic value. We cannot argue that God exists because an event is an act of God. For unless there is already a God who can act, there cannot be an act of God. In short, either the alleged miraculous event is known to be such because it is part of a supernatural system (which begs the question), or else we must be able to identify the event as supernatural from a strictly naturalistic perspective. But according to Flew, this is impossible, since an unusual event in the natural realm is, from a strictly naturalistic perspective, a strictly natural event.

The Second Statement of Flew's Argument

The heart of Flew's argument now comes into focus.[14] Miracles are not identifiable, because there is no way to define them without begging the question. The reasoning proceeds thus:

1. A miracle must be identifiable before it can be identified.
2. A miracle is identified in only one of two ways—either as an unusual event in nature, or as an exception to nature.
3. But an unusual event in nature is simply a natural event, not a miracle.

14. Ibid., pp. 348–49.

4. And an exception to nature cannot be known (i.e., identified) from within nature alone.
5. Therefore, a miracle is not identifiable.

And, of course, what is not identifiable has no evidential value. That
is, it cannot be used to prove anything, as many Christians do to
prove the truth of Christianity.

A Response to Flew's Argument

It would seem that Flew has made a penetrating point. His first
premise is solid. We must know what we are looking for before we
can ever know we have found it. If we cannot define it, then we cannot be sure we have discovered it.

There is no way to define miracles in terms of natural events, for
then miracles would be reduced to natural events. To define them
in terms of a supernatural cause (God), however, is to suppose that
God exists. Therefore, miracles cannot be used as an evidence of
God's existence; they presuppose the existence of God. In short, the
supernaturalist argues in a circle.

First Response: Presuppose God's Existence

One way to reply to Flew is to claim that arguing in a circle is not
unique to supernaturalists, since naturalists do the same thing. For
antisupernaturalist arguments presuppose naturalism. Thus, some
theists simply claim that it is necessary to argue in a circle. They insist
that all reason is circular.[15] For in the final analysis, all thought is
grounded in faith.

If supernaturalists choose to go this route, their grounds (or lack
of grounds) are just as good as those of the antisupernaturalists.
Certainly naturalists who attempt to rule out miracles on the basis
of a faith commitment to naturalism are in no position to forbid theists from simply believing that God exists and, hence, that miracles
are possible and identifiable. Once naturalists are granted the privi-
lege of a mere belief basis for naturalism, for which they have no
rational or scientific proof, then in all fairness we must allow other
alternate worldviews the same opportunity.

15. Cornelius Van Til, *Defense of the Faith* (Philadelphia: Presbyterian and
Reformed, 1955), p. 118.

Second Response: Offer Evidence for God's Existence

There is, however, another avenue of approach open to theists: theists may offer some rational justification for belief in God. If successful, then they can define (show the identifiability of) miracles in terms of the supernatural realm they have reason to think exists. The following is offered as an example of such an approach.

By rational justification is meant a sound argument. Sound arguments are made up of only true premises from which a valid conclusion is drawn. The following premises of the argument are all apparently true. How they are known to be true and with what degree of certainty is unimportant here as long as it is reasonable to believe they are true. It is noteworthy to point out, however, that even nontheists generally hold them to be true. These premises are as follows:

1. Something exists.
2. Nothing cannot cause something; only something can cause something.
3. The effect cannot be greater than its cause.[16]

All three premises are accepted as true by most people without serious question. The first one is undeniably true, since we cannot consistently deny that everything exists including ourselves. We must exist before we can deny that anything exists.

The second premise is obviously true as well. The popular song "Nothing comes from nothing; nothing ever could" reflects the widespread belief in the truth of this statement. Even Hume wrote, "I never asserted so absurd a proposition that anything might arise without a cause."[17] It seems obvious enough that absolutely nothing has absolutely no power to cause anything. It is a fundamental presupposition of scientific exploration that "every event has a cause." While it may be logically possible that something may just "arise" or "come to be" without a cause, it is contrary to our experience and is counterintuitive. All rational people respect this kind of belief in their ordinary life and thought.

16. For a more detailed statement of an argument for God's existence, see Norman L. Geisler, *Christian Apologetics* (Grand Rapids: Baker, 1976), chap. 13. For an example of a debate about issues regarding theism and miracles, see J. P. Moreland and Kai Nielsen, *Does God Exist? The Great Debate* (Nashville: Thomas Nelson, 1990).

17. David Hume, *The Letters of David Hume*, ed. J. Y. T. Greig (Oxford: Oxford University Press, 1932), 1:187.

The third premise is also an almost universally accepted truth. The popular adage "It takes one to make one" is evidence of the widely accepted truth that effects resemble their causes in some significant way. Likewise, "Water can rise no higher than its source" is one way to affirm that the cause must in some significant sense be at least equal to the effect (although not necessarily in every way). Computers, for example, do not resemble their creators in every way, but what they are programmed to do is no better than their programmer. Thus it is not legitimate to point to a student's exam and say that it bears no significant resemblance to the pen that produced those marks on the paper. For there is only an accidental relationship between the pen (which is only an instrumental cause of the exam) and the exam.

On the other hand, there is an essential relationship between the student's mind (the efficient cause of the exam) and the exam. It is in this latter sense that an effect resembles its efficient cause. For instance, malaria does not resemble mosquitoes, since mosquitoes are not the cause of the disease but only the carriers. Malaria parasites do resemble malaria parasites in significant and essential ways, because they are the cause of other parasites that resemble them. Likewise, musicians give birth to nonmusicians; this special ability is only accidental to their humanity. But humans give birth to humans; that is an essential similarity.

Now granting that these premises are true—and it seems reasonable to believe that they are—then all that remains is to put them together in a valid way for the resulting argument to be a sound one. That is, a valid conclusion from true premises will yield a true conclusion. The following is a widely held theistic argument based on these three premises.

If something exists and if nothing cannot cause something, then it follows that something must necessarily and eternally exist. It must exist eternally since, if nothing ever was, then nothing could now be. But something undeniably now is. Therefore, something always has been. Likewise, something must always have been because nothing cannot cause something. But if something is and if nothing cannot cause something, then it follows that something must necessarily always have been. And, since the cause must bear some significant similarity to its effect, which is an intelligent moral being, then it is reasonable to posit an intelligent, moral cause of everything else that exists. If this is so, then the theistic argument for God is sound. And if God exists, then there is a supernatural realm by which a supernatural event can be identified in the natural world.

In any event—whether by proof or by mere postulate of God—theists can answer Flew's basic challenge of the identifiability of the miraculous by referring the distinctive characteristics of a miracle to a supernatural Being, God. If such a God exists, and we know something about what he is like, then his "fingerprints" (miracles) are not only possible, they are identifiable.

Nature is certainly the backdrop for the miraculous. Without regular natural laws, irregular miracles would not be possible. Furthermore, a miracle needs to be identified (defined) before we could know that one has occurred. Flew does make a good point when he insists that there is no legitimate way to define a miracle, except in terms of a supernatural realm. It certainly cannot be defined in terms of what happens regularly. For then by definition it would be a natural event.

Flew's challenge can be met in one of two ways. Theists can simply presuppose God, who is defined by certain supernatural characteristics, or they can offer a proof for such a God. We have shown how both can be done. In either case we have met the need to show that the existence of God is logically prior to the very definition and identification of miracles. Only if a God who can act exists, can we identify an alleged miraculous event as an act of God.

6

ARE MIRACLES MYTHOLOGICAL?

The canon "If miraculous, unhistorical" is one they bring to
their study of the texts, not one they have learned from it.
—C. S. Lewis

UNDER THE RELENTLESS ATTACK of modern naturalists, many religious
thinkers have retreated to the view that miracles are not events in the
space-time world. Rather, miracles are myths or events in a spiritual
world, above space and time. As a consequence, the religious records
must be "demythologized" or divested of their mythological "husk"
to get at the existential "kernel" of truth. Rudolf Bultmann is at the
forefront of this view of "miracles." He adapts phenomenologist
Martin Heidegger's concept of existential analysis to New Testament
exegesis. Using this methodology, he attempts to separate the essential gospel message from the first-century worldview.

Bultmann's Demythological Naturalism

According to Bultmann, "the cosmology of the New Testament is
essentially mythical in character." By this he means "the world is
viewed as a three-storied structure, with the earth in the centre, the
heaven above, and the underworld beneath." The world "is the
scene of the supernatural activity of God and his angels on the one
hand, and of Satan and his demons on the other. These supernatural
forces intervene in the course of nature and in all that we think and
will and do."[1]

1. Rudolf Bultmann, *Kerygma and Myth: A Theological Debate*, ed. Hans Werner
Bartsch, trans. Reginald H. Fuller (London: Billing and Sons, 1954), p. 1.

The New Testament, says Bultmann, presents its redemptive story in a miraculous, mythological form. "God sent forth his Son, a pre-existent divine Being who appears on earth as a man. He dies the death of a sinner on the cross. . . . His resurrection marks the beginning of the cosmic catastrophe. . . . The risen Christ is exalted to the right hand of God in heaven and made 'Lord' and 'King.'"[2]

Bultmann believes that "all this is the language of mythology . . . to this extent the kerygma is incredible to modern man, for he is convinced that the mythical view of the world is obsolete." In view of this he asks "whether, when we preach the Gospel today, we expect our converts to accept . . . the mythical view of the world in which it is set. If not does the New Testament embody a truth which is quite independent of its mythical setting?" And "if it does, theology must undertake the task of stripping the Kerygma [proclamation] from its mythical framework, 'demythologizing' it."[3]

Many Christians insist that modern people must accept belief of the miraculous along with the message of the gospel, but for Bultmann this is both senseless and impossible. "It would be senseless, because there is nothing specifically Christian in the mythical view of the world as such. It is simply the cosmology of a pre-scientific age." Further, "it would be impossible, because no man can adopt a view of the world by his own volition—it is already determined for him by his place in history." The reason for this, says Bultmann, is that "all our thinking to-day is shaped for good or ill by modern science." So "a blind acceptance of the New Testament mythology would be irrational. . . . It would involve a sacrifice of the intellect. . . . It would mean accepting a view of the world in our faith and religion which we should deny in our everyday life."[4]

With unlimited confidence, then, Bultmann pronounces the biblical picture of miracles as impossible. For "man's knowledge and mastery of the world have advanced to such an extent through science and technology that it is no longer possible for anyone seriously to hold the New Testament view of the world—in fact, there is hardly anyone who does." Therefore, the only honest way of reciting the creeds is to strip the mythological framework from the truth they enshrine. For "now that the forces and the laws of nature have been

2. Ibid., p. 2. For a discussion of Rudolf Bultmann's antisupernaturalism, see Ronald Nash, *Christian Faith and Historical Understanding* (Dallas, Tex.: Probe/Word, 1990), chap. 4.

3. Ibid., p. 3.

4. Ibid., pp. 3–4.

discovered, we can no longer believe in spirits, whether good or evil."[5] It is simply "impossible to use electric light and the wireless and to avail ourselves of modern medical and surgical discoveries, and at the same time to believe in the New Testament world of demons and spirits."[6] Therefore, concludes Bultmann, "the only relevant . . . assumption is the view of the world which has been molded by modern science and the modern conception of human nature as a self-subsistent unity immune from the interference of supernatural powers."[7] This means that "the resurrection of Jesus is just as difficult, it means an event whereby a supernatural power is released. . . . To the biologists such language is meaningless . . . such a notion [the idealist] finds intolerable."[8]

If the biblical picture is mythological, how then are we to understand it? For Bultmann "the real purpose of myth is not to present an objective picture of the world as it is, but to express man's understanding of himself in the world in which he lives." Therefore "myth should be interpreted not cosmologically, but anthropologically, or better still, existentially." That is, "myth speaks of the power or the powers which man supposes he experiences as the ground and limit of his world and of his own activity and suffering." In other words, "the real purpose of myth is to speak of a transcendent power which controls the world and man, but that purpose is impeded and obscured by the terms in which it is expressed."[9]

Unlike the older liberal theologians who "used criticism to eliminate the mythology of the New Testament, our task to-day," notes Bultmann, "is to use criticism to interpret it."[10] How far does this criticism lead Bultmann? Was the Christ of the New Testament a mere mythical figure? Bultmann's answer is No. "He is also a concrete figure of history—Jesus of Nazareth. His life is more than a mythical event; it is a human life which ended in the tragedy of crucifixion. We have here a unique combination of history and myth."[11] The miracles and resurrection of Christ, however, are another matter. They are not historical but suprahistorical events.

5. Ibid., p. 4.
6. Ibid., p. 5.
7. Ibid.
8. Ibid., p. 8.
9. Ibid., pp. 10–11.
10. Ibid., p. 12.
11. Ibid., p. 34.

Bultmann concludes confidently, "Obviously [the resurrection] is not an event of past history. . . . An historical fact which involves a resurrection from the dead is utterly inconceivable."[12] He offers several reasons for this antisupernatural conclusion. First, there is "the incredibility of a mythical event like the resuscitation of a corpse—for that is what the resurrection means." Second, "there is the difficulty of establishing the objective historicity of the resurrection no matter how many witnesses are cited, as though once it was established it might be believed beyond all question and faith might have its unimpeachable guarantee." Third, "the resurrection is an article of faith. . . . So it cannot be a miraculous proof." Finally, "such a miracle is not otherwise unknown to mythology."[13]

In view of this, Bultmann says, it is "abundantly clear that the New Testament is interested in the resurrection of Christ simply and solely because it is the eschatological event par excellence."[14] Hence, "if the event of Easter Day is in any sense an historical event additional to the event of the cross, it is nothing else than the rise of faith in the risen Lord. . . . All that historical criticism can establish is the fact that the first disciples came to believe in the resurrection."[15]

What then is the resurrection, if not an event of objective space-time history? For Bultmann, it is an event of subjective history, for "the historical problem is scarcely relevant to Christian belief in the Resurrection. For the historical event of the rise of the Easter faith means for us . . . the act of God in which the redemptive event of the cross is completed."[16] It is an event of subjective history, an event of faith in the hearts of the early disciples. As such, these "miracles" are not subject to objective historical verification or falsification, for they are not really events in the space-time world. Christ did not rise from Joseph's tomb, but by faith in the disciples' hearts.

It is obvious even to the casual reader that Bultmann is opposed to the miracles of the Bible, including the resurrection of Christ. Before evaluating his conclusions, we will restate Bultmann's central claim.

In view of his rigid naturalistic presuppositions, it is not surprising that Bultmann engages in a demythologizing of the Gospel record. What is of central importance here is his conclusion that

12. Ibid., pp. 38–39.
13. Ibid., pp. 39–40.
14. Ibid., p. 40.
15. Ibid.
16. Ibid.

"miracles" are by nature suprahistorical, that they are not events in the space-time world. It is difficult to formulate precisely what reasoning Bultmann uses to support this thesis. It seems to go like this:

1. Myths are by nature more than objective truths; they are transcendent truths of faith.
2. But what is not objective cannot be part of a verifiable space-time world.
3. Therefore, miracles (myths) are not part of the objective space-time world.

An Evaluation of Demythological Naturalism

In view of Bultmann's view of the miraculous, several objections can be offered. First, it does not follow that because an event is more than historical it must be less than historical. Gospel miracles, to be sure, have a "moreness" or transcendent dimension. They cannot be reduced to mere historical events. For example, the virgin birth is more than biological; it points to the divine nature of Christ and to the spiritual purpose of his mission. It is not merely a matter of science; it is also presented as a "sign" (Isa. 7:14). The same is true of Christ's resurrection. Although it is at least that, it is portrayed as more than a mere resuscitation of a corpse. It has a divine dimension that entails spiritual truths as well (Rom. 4:25; 2 Tim. 1:10).

But having said all this, we are by no means bound to conclude that because these miracles are presented as more than the purely objective and factual, they are not at least objective and factual events. Even Bultmann admits that the New Testament writers believed these events to be historical: "It cannot be denied that the resurrection of Jesus is often used in the New Testament as a miraculous proof . . . [but] both the legend of the empty tomb and the appearances insist on the physical reality of the risen body of the Lord." Bultmann adds, however, that "these are most certainly later embellishments of the primitive tradition."[17] Apart from simply presupposing the scientific "unacceptability" of these miracles to "modern" people (which is a questionable assumption),[18] there are no solid reasons for concluding that these events could not be events in space-time history.

17. Ibid., p. 39.
18. See the discussion in chap. 4.

Second, simply because an event is not *of* the world does not mean that it cannot occur *in* the world. That is, a miracle can originate out of the supernatural world (its source) and yet it can occur in the natural world (its sphere). In this way the event can be objective and verifiable without being reducible to its purely factual dimensions. Thus we could verify directly by historical means whether the corpse of Jesus of Nazareth was raised and empirically observed (the objective dimensions of the miracle), without reducing the spiritual aspects of the event to mere scientific data. But in claiming that miracles such as the resurrection cannot occur in space-time history, Bultmann is merely revealing an unjustified, dogmatic, naturalistic bias.

Third, it is evident that the basis of Bultmann's antisupernaturalism is not evidential, nor even open to real discussion. It is something he holds no matter how many witnesses are cited. The dogmatism of his language is revealing. Miracles are "incredible," "irrational," "no longer possible," "meaningless," "utterly inconceivable," "simply impossible," "intolerable." Hence, the "only honest way" for modern people is to hold that miracles are "nothing else than spiritual" and that the physical world is "immune from interference" in a supernatural way. This is not the language of one open to historical evidence for a miracle. It looks more like a mind that does not wish to be "confused" with the facts!

Fourth, if miracles are not objective historical events, then they are unverifiable or unfalsifiable. That is, there is no factual way to determine their truth or falsity. But if this is so, then they have been placed beyond the realm of objective truth and must be treated as purely subjective and unverifiable. If so, then Flew's criticism is to the point: "Now it often seems to people who are not religious as if there was no conceivable event or series of events the occurrence of which would be admitted by sophisticated religious people to be a sufficient reason for conceding 'There wasn't a God after all.' . . . What would have to occur or to have occurred to constitute for you a disproof of the love of, or of the existence of, God?"[19]

Let us rephrase this question for Bultmann: "If the corpse of Jesus of Nazareth had been discovered after the first Easter, would this falsify your belief in the resurrection?" His answer is clearly No. By contrast the answer of the apostle Paul is clearly Yes. For "if Christ

19. Antony Flew, "Theology and Falsification," in *New Essays in Philosophical Theology* (London: SCM, 1963), p. 98.

has not been raised, your faith is futile; you are still in your sins" (1 Cor. 15:17). Therefore, it is obvious that Bultmann's understanding of miracles is contrary to that found in one of the earliest known Christian records of these events, the New Testament.[20]

Furthermore, if miracles are not historical events, then they have no evidential value. Nothing can be proved by them since they have value only for those who wish to believe them. The New Testament writers, however, claim evidential value for miracles. They consider them "convincing proofs" (Acts 1:3) and not "cleverly devised myths" (2 Pet. 1:16 RSV). Paul declares that "God has given proof of this to all men by raising him [Jesus] from the dead" (Acts 17:31).

Finally, Bultmann's demythologizing approach to the New Testament documents is unjustified for several reasons. First and foremost, it is contrary to the overwhelming evidence for the authenticity of the New Testament documents and the reliability of the witnesses (see chap. 12). Second, it is contrary to the New Testament claim for itself not to be "cleverly invented myths" (2 Pet. 1:16) but an eye-witness account (cf. John 21:24; 1 John 1:1–3). Finally, the New Testament is not the literary genre of mythology. One great Oxford scholar, himself a writer of myth (fairytales), notes that "Dr. Bultmann never wrote a gospel." He asks, therefore, "Has the experience of his learned . . . life really given him any power of seeing into the minds of those long dead [who have]?" Bultmannian biblical critiques are unfalsifiable because, as Lewis wryly remarks, "St. Mark is dead. When they meet St. Peter there will be more pressing matters to discuss."[21]

Bultmann accommodates the modern trend against miracles by insisting that miracles are mythological but not historical. They embody a spiritual truth that must be demythologized from the legend. This spiritual or existential truth, however, is not an observable space-time event. It is an event of faith. Christ, for example, did not rise bodily from the tomb; he simply arose by faith in the disciples' hearts on the first Easter. In brief, miracles are not historical but

20. First Corinthians is widely accepted, even by biblical critics, as the work of the apostle Paul, dating ca. A.D. 55 or 56.

21. C. S. Lewis, *Christian Reflections* (Grand Rapids: Eerdmans, 1967), pp. 161–63. For a detailed discussion of failed attempts to discredit the incarnation and resurrection by treating them as pagan beliefs, see Ronald Nash, *Christianity and the Hellenistic World* (Dallas, Tex.: Probe/Word, 1991).

suprahistorical. They are not events in the space-time world. Therefore, they cannot be objectively verified.

In response to Bultmann's assertions, several things have been pointed out. First, simply because miracles are more than historical does not mean they are less than historical. Second, miracles can be events *in* the world and yet not be *of* the world. Further, Bultmann's use of words such as "simply impossible" and "utterly inconceivable" shows that he is not really approaching the topic historically but dogmatically. Finally, Bultmann's view is objectively unverifiable and unfalsifiable.

Whether miracles have occurred in the world cannot be decided by philosophical dogma. It is a matter of historical research. But to say with Bultmann that miracles are purely suprahistorical myths not observable in the space-time world is to reject traditional Judaism and Christianity. And to demythologize in the name of Christianity is a vain attempt at reconciliation by capitulation.

ARE MIRACLES HISTORICAL?

> Copies which had been as universally received and acted upon
> as the Four Gospels, would have been received in evidence in
> any court of justice, without the slightest hesitation.—Simon
> Greenleaf

WHATEVER ELSE WE MAY THINK of them, biblical miracles claim to be historical, not suprahistorical, events. If this is the case, the question arises as to whether these miracles, as space-time events, are a proper subject of historical research. Some have argued that if the nature of miracles is understood to be historical, then the nature of the historical method renders miracles historically unknowable.

Serious issues rest in the balance here. First, if miracles are not historical, then the whole fabric of orthodox Jewish and Christian belief is false. This means that the traditional understanding of everything from the story of Adam and Eve to the healings of Jesus is false. What is more, it also means that Christian belief is at its heart objectively unverifiable. It is a subjective matter of belief not based on objective miraculous facts.

Miracle History Is Unknowable

Troeltsch's Principles of Analogy

In his famous principles of historiography, German theologian Ernst Troeltsch lays down the rule of analogy: The only way we can know the past is by analogies in the present. The unknown is arrived at only through the known. "On the analogy of the events known

75

to us we seek by conjecture and sympathetic understanding to explain and reconstruct the past." Without uniformity of the present and the past, we could not know anything from the past. For without analogies from the present we cannot understand the past.[1]

On the basis of this principle, some have insisted that "no amount of testimony is ever permitted to establish as past reality a thing that cannot be found in present reality." Even if "the witness may have a perfect character—all that goes for nothing."[2] This would mean that, unless we can identify miracles (such as are found in the New Testament) in the present, we have no reason to believe that they occurred in the past. English philosopher F. H. Bradley states the problem this way:

> We have seen that history rests in the last resort upon an inference from our experience, a judgment based upon our own present state of things; . . . when we are asked to affirm the existence in past time of events, the effects of causes which confessedly are without analogy in the world in which we live, and which we know—we are at a loss for any answer but this, that . . . we are asked to build a house without a foundation. . . . And how can we attempt this without contradicting ourselves?[3]

Since it is widely believed that miracles such as the virgin birth, walking on water, and raising the dead are no longer occurring today, then it would follow (by Troeltsch's analogy) that such events cannot be known to have happened in history. In short, biblical miracles are historically unknowable.

Flew's "Critical History"

According to Flew, "critical history" is based on two principles stated by Hume.[4]

---

1. Ernst Troeltsch, "Historiography," in *Encyclopedia of Religion and Ethics* (New York: Charles Scribner's Sons, 1955), 6:718.

2. Carl Becker, "Detachment and the Writing of History," in *Detachment and the Writing of History*, ed. Phil L. Snyder (Westport, Conn.: Greenwood, 1972), pp. 12–13.

3. F. H. Bradley, *The Presuppositions of Critical History* (Chicago: Quadrangle, 1968), p. 100.

4. See Hume, *Treatise* 2.3.1; *Inquiry* 8.

1. "The present detritus [remains] of the past cannot be interpreted as historical evidence at all, unless we presume that
   the same basic regularities obtained then as today."
2. "The historian must employ as criteria all his present knowledge, or presumed knowledge, of what is probable or
   improbable, possible or impossible."[5]

Now, writes Flew, "it is only and precisely by presuming that the
laws that hold today held in the past . . . that we can rationally interpret the detritus of the past as evidence and from it construct our
account of what actually happened."[6]

In the light of this discussion, Flew concludes that "the critical
historian, confronted with some story of a miracle, will usually dismiss it out of hand."[7] When asked "to justify his procedure, he will
have to appeal to precisely the principle which Hume advanced: the
'absolute impossibility or miraculous nature' of the events attested
must, 'in the eyes of all reasonable people . . . alone be regarded as a
sufficient refutation.'"[8] This impossibility, Flew adds quickly, is not
logical but physical. Miracles are possible in principle, but in practice the historian must always reject them. For the very nature of the
historical method demands that the past be interpreted in accordance
with the (naturalistic) regularities of the present.

We may now summarize the premises of Flew's argument and
begin to analyze it.

1. All critical history depends on the validity of two principles:
   (a) The remains of the past can be used as evidence for
   reconstructing history only if we presume the same basic
   regularities of nature held then as now; and (b) the critical
   historian must use the present knowledge of the possible
   and probable as criteria for knowing the past.
2. But belief in miracles is contrary to both of these principles.
3. Therefore, belief in miracles is contrary to critical history.

Conversely, only naive and uncritical persons can believe in miracles.
For the past can be known only in terms of the regular patterns of

5. Antony Flew, "Miracles," in *Encyclopedia of Philosophy*, ed. Paul Edwards (New
York: Macmillan, 1967), 5:350.
6. Ibid., p. 351.
7. Ibid., p. 352.
8. Ibid.

the present. And these patterns of nature in the present rule out any knowledge of miracles in the past.

An Evaluation of the Historical Argument Against Miracles

First, this argument does not claim to eliminate the *possibility* of miracles. It simply attempts to rule out their *knowability* by what Flew calls "critical history." Further, as Flew admits, the argument follows the basic form of Hume's antisupernaturalism. That is to say, it assumes that to be truly critical and historical one must be antisupernatural. On the contrary, one would think that a truly critical mind would not be closed to any possibility to which the evidence actually pointed.

There are a number of fallacies involved in the above argument. Let us note several of importance.

Special pleading. The first problem is that Flew's argument engages in special pleading. Flew is not willing to allow evidence to count for any particular events, such as miracles, in view of the evidence for events in general. That is, since there are far more regular and repeatable events than the special and unrepeatable kind (miracles), this fact is used to argue that the particular event counts as no real evidence at all. In effect, Flew is adding evidence for other like events, rather than weighing evidence for a particular event. It is like refusing to believe that I have won the lottery, simply because there are thousands more who have lost!

Flew special pleads in another way. He assumes without proof that there are no miracles in the present. Maybe there are and maybe there are not; that is beside the point.[9] But Flew must show there are none and not simply assume it. For if there are miracles in the present, then we would possess the needed analogy for knowing the past.

Begging the question. Flew also commits the fallacy of *petitio principii,* for in practice he admits that miracles are "absolutely impossible" and that critical thinkers will dismiss them "out of hand." But why should critical thinkers be so biased against the historical reality of a miracle? Why should they begin with a methodology loaded against certain kinds of events occurring in the past, before they ever look at the evidence for them?

9. See chaps. 11–12; Norman L. Geisler, *Signs and Wonders* (Wheaton: Tyndale, 1988) for a discussion of current miracle claims.

Historical uniformitarianism. Another way to state this objection is that Flew has adopted a historical uniformitarianism. He begins by assuming that all past events are uniformly the same as present ones.[10] This is not only a mere assumption, but it is contrary to the belief of these naturalistic scientists (and of most scientists) about origins. For scientists believe that the origin of the universe and the origin of life are singular and unrepeatable events.[11] But if the past can be known only in terms of the processes of the present, then there would be no scientific basis for knowledge about these origins, since they are singular and unrepeatable events of the past. Such an assumption is harmful to scientific progress, as the next point will illustrate.

Confusion of uniformity (analogy) and uniformitarianism. Another way to state the issue is to point to a confusion in Flew's argument between the legitimate principle of uniformity (analogy) and the illegitimate use of uniformitarianism. Besides having a built-in naturalistic bias, uniformitarianism assumes wrongly that because the basis for knowing the past is regularly occurring events in the present, that the object in the past cannot be a singularity. It is clear that this does not follow. An archeologist, for example, may know on the basis of regular experience in the present that only intelligent beings can make things like arrowheads. This does not mean, however, that the archeologist cannot know (by analogy) that the object of a search (say, a single arrowhead) was produced by an intelligent being in the past.

Likewise, the SETI (Search for Extra-Terrestrial Intelligence) is believed to be scientific for believing that receipt of a single message from space will reveal the existence of intelligent life. For even if the object of pursuit is the reception of only one message, nevertheless, the basis of knowing that it was produced by intelligence is the regular conjunction of intelligent beings with this kind of complex information.[12] So, while knowledge of the past is based on analogies

10. There is a parallel here in the science of geology, which long overlooked the fact that many past processes were catastrophic and much faster than those observed in the present.

11. For further discussion of this point, see Norman L. Geisler, *Origin Science* (Grand Rapids: Baker, 1987), chap. 7.

12. By "complex information" we mean what microbiologists call "specified complexity." Crystals, for example, have a message that is specified but not complex. Random polymers, on the other hand, have a message that is complex but not specified. But the DNA message in living things is both specified and complex. This same kind of specified complexity exists in written languages and is identifiable by the letter sequences. See Herbert Yockey, "Self-organization Origin of Life Scenarios and Information Theory," *Journal of Theoretical Biology* 91 (1981): 13.

in the present (uniformity), the object of this knowledge can be a singularity.

A hindrance to scientific progress. Hindering views are evident in the thinking of some of the most brilliant minds of modern science. Robert Jastrow notes that "There is a kind of religion in science; it is the religion of a person who believes . . . every event can be explained in a rational way as the product of some previous event."[13] The problem with this, declares Jastrow, is that this scientific "religious faith" is being upset by scientific discoveries.

The Big Bang theory of the origin of the universe is a case in point. As pointed out in chapter 1, Eddington spoke of this nonuniform, special, explosive beginning of the universe as "repugnant," "preposterous," and "incredible."[14] The German chemist Walter Nernst wrote, "To deny the infinite duration of time [with a Big Bang beginning] would be to betray the very foundations of science."[15] After Einstein made a mistake in mathematics attempting to refute the Big Bang theory, he admitted it was because the evidence pointed to a conclusion he was uncomfortable with at the time. Even Stephen Hawking, who earlier admitted the strong evidence in favor of it, is now proposing a more speculative alternative.[16]

In brief, the presupposition that the past operates with the same unbroken processes as the present is apparently false. The evidence shows that the process by which the universe came to be is unique.[17] Many scientists believe that the basic hydrogen atoms of the universe were created in milliseconds. Many astronomers today believe the universe began with a great explosion (several billions of years ago). But there is nothing like this occurring in the present! Therefore, on Flew's basis, we would have to reject out of hand this modern scientific theory of the origin of the universe, simply because we have no like events today.

But what if the Big Bang theory is ultimately proven to be false in favor of some other theory, such as a rebound or cyclical theory?[18] It does not matter for our purposes here for two reasons. First, it was still considered to be a viable theory of origins held by many reputable scientists, the object of which was an unrepeated singularity. But if

13. Robert Jastrow, *God and the Astronomers* (New York: Norton, 1978), p. 113.
14. Ibid., p. 112.
15. Ibid.
16. See Stephen Hawking, *A Brief History of Time* (New York: Bantam, 1988).
17. Ibid., p. 27.
18. Ibid.

this kind of singularity can be considered the proper object of historical science, then there is no reason that miracles should be ruled out as the object of history. Further, there is a singularity admitted by all that will not be falsified. As C. S. Lewis notes, the history of the universe happened only once, and yet it is an unrepeated singularity.[19]

Appealing to the general to rule out a particular event. There is a strange sort of logic going on in Flew's argument. It amounts to claiming that we must judge all particular (special) events in the past on the basis of general (regular) events in the present. But why should we do this? Why not use special events in the present as an analogy for special events in the past? There are unique and particular events in the present. Scientists call them anomalies. From a strictly scientific point of view a miracle is like an anomaly. Of course, miracles have other characteristics (theological and moral ones) that an anomaly does not (see chap. 9). But all we need to do for a meaningful understanding of a past miracle (assuming none exist in the present) is to combine the anomalous with the moral-theological characteristics known about God and the result is an understanding of what is meant by a miracle.

Along these same lines, the contemporary philosopher Douglas K. Erlandson argues that scientific law as such is concerned with types of events (i.e., with general classes of events), whereas the supernaturalist is concerned with exceptions (particular events that do not fit into general classes). And a belief in the latter does not upset a belief in the former.[20] To put this in Flew's terms, we can believe that the "basic regularities" of the present did indeed obtain in the past, without insisting there were absolutely no exceptions to these regular patterns (or types) in the past. Only when we overstep the observation of and scientific basis for natural law and insist that the "regularities" were really absolute uniformities can the knowability of miracles be eliminated.

It proves too much. Another way to state the problem in Flew's reasoning is to note that his argument proves too much—it proves that much of what he and other naturalists believe about the past cannot be true. As Richard Whately shows in his satire on Hume's naturalistic skepticism,[21] if we must reject unique events in the past

19. C. S. Lewis, *Miracles* (New York: Macmillan, 1947).

20. Douglas K. Erlandson, "A New Look," *Religious Studies* 3/4 (Dec. 1977): 417–28.

21. Richard Whately, *Historical Doubts Relative to Napoleon Bonaparte* (New York: Robert Caster and Brothers, 1949), pp. 224, 290.

because there is no analogy in the present, then we would have to conclude that the accepted history of Napoleon—with its incredible and unique military exploits—is also untrue.

It is not critical enough. Flew's approach to history does not criticize the uncritical, unreasonable acceptance of presuppositions that eliminate valid historical knowledge. Far from being open to evidence, Flew's naturalism eliminates in advance any miraculous interpretation of events in the past. In effect, it legislates meaning rather than looks for it. He claims to know in advance what these past events must mean, rather than seeking to understand what they do mean.

Following principles of historical interpretation laid down by Hume and Troeltsch, some modern naturalists have argued that miracles are historically unknowable. This is so, they say, because the past can be known only in terms of the present, and the present operates in a regular (uniform) way. In response, it has been shown that this argument engages in special pleading and begging the question in favor of naturalism.

Furthermore, if this historical uniformitarianism is accepted, it will hinder scientific progress. In addition to this, we can maintain the regularity of the past and its similarity to the present and still admit to some (miraculous) exceptions to this regular pattern. Finally, contrary to the naturalistic historian, the truly "critical" mind should not legislate the meaning of past events; it should look for their true meaning whether this is natural or supernatural.

The implication, then, is that Christian claims are historically verifiable. It is not simply a matter of subjective belief. We can examine the records of the past and, by rational means, determine whether certain Christian claims are true or false.

ARE MIRACLES ESSENTIAL?

And if Christ is not risen, your faith is futile; you are still in your sins!—St. Paul

THOMAS HOBBES BELIEVED that miracles were contrary to human reason, and only commended them tongue-in-cheek. Immanuel Kant found miracles neither essential for faith nor necessary for the essence of true religion. Indeed, even if miracles have occurred, many devoutly religious people have denied that they are really necessary to religion. Many of the great religious minds in the modern world have followed this approach to the miracles question. Their reasons provide a significant argument for naturalism.

Again, if these men are right, traditional Christianity and Judaism are wrong, since both use miracles as a support of the very heart of their belief. Likewise, much of modern religious belief is misdirected with its emphasis on supernatural conversions and miraculous prophecies about the future.

Indeed, if miracles are not essential to true religion, we should be content with normal religious experience common to humankind, making no claim to unique divine confirmation of any religious experience.

Miracles Are Not Essential to True Religion

Spinoza insisted that miracles were not only unhelpful to true religion but actually harmful to it. He declared that all that is essential to true religion is basically moral. The whole of the Protestant tra-

83

dition following Schleiermacher, the father of modern religious liberalism, adopted this basic stance as well.[1] Hobbes and Kant were also early proponents of this view.

Thomas Hobbes: Miracles Can Be Harmful to Religion

One of the major forces in early British empiricism, Hobbes (1588–1679) was a well trained classicist and logician. He combined empirical and rationalistic methods in a naturalistic form of materialism. One of the ramifications of his system was a "natural" religion that denies any role to the supernatural in our world.

Hobbes' "natural religion" was a much more subtle denunciation of miracles than was Spinoza's pantheism. In fact, his denial was cast in the form of a tongue-in-cheek "defense" of the Christian religion. Satire was a much safer form of denial in a day of religious intolerance.

According to Hobbes, the origin of natural religion is found in four things: "opinion of ghosts, ignorance of second causes, devotion towards what men fear, and taking of things casual for prognostics."[2] That is, people attribute things to supernatural causes when they do not know the natural causes. "For the way by which they think these invisible agents wrought their effects [is through] men that know not what it is that we call causing."[3] If people knew the natural cause, they would not attribute a supernatural one to it.

Probably with tongue in cheek, Hobbes claims the situation is much better for the supernaturally revealed religion of Christianity, the official state religion of his day. For "where God himself by supernatural revelation planted religion, there he also made to himself a peculiar kingdom." The basis of this kind of religion "can be no other than the operation of miracles, or true prophecy (which also is a miracle)." Of course, "that which taketh away the reputation of wisdom in him that formeth a religion . . . is the enjoining of a belief of contradictories . . . and therefore to enjoin the belief of them is an argument of ignorance." Likewise, "that which taketh away the reputation of sincerity is the doing or saying of such things as appear to be signs that what they require other men to believe is not believed by themselves." All of this is scandalous and along with the "injustice, cruelty, profaneness,

1. See Friedrich Schleiermacher, *On Religion: Speeches to Its Cultured Despisers*, trans. John Oman (New York: Harper Torchbooks, 1958); Adolf Harnack, *What Is Christianity?* trans. Thomas B. Saunders (New York: Harper Torchbooks, 1957).

2. Thomas Hobbes, *Leviathan*, in *Great Books of the Western World*, ed. Robert M. Hutchins (Chicago: Encyclopedia Britannica, 1952), 23:80.

3. Ibid.

avarice, and luxury" of those who propound such miracles, there is a stumbling block of those who would believe.[4]

But while Hobbes pays homage to the alleged supernatural basis of the Christian religion, he also undermines it. For besides the serious doubts, both of natural and revealed religion, that he casts on the belief in supernatural causes, Hobbes offers a subtle argument against the usefulness of miracles. Noting the apostasy of the people in biblical times after the great prophets had performed their mighty miracles, Hobbes adds, "So that miracles failing, faith also failed."[5] Miracles are not really that helpful after all. For as soon as they disappear so does the faith they were intended to arouse.

On the basis of his materialistic understanding of the world, Hobbes engages in some desupernaturalizing of the Gospel record. He boldly proclaims that "the Scriptures by the Spirit of God in man mean a man's spirit, inclined to godliness."[6] As to the story of Jesus casting a demon out of a man, Hobbes sees "nothing at all in the Scripture that requireth a belief that demoniacs were any other thing but madmen."[7] By implication the whole Gospel record could be desupernaturalized.

For Hobbes, miracles are not essential and probably not even helpful to religion. What is essential to religion is faith. Claiming that "natural reason" is the "undoubted word of God," Hobbes insists that in the religious realm we must live by "the will of obedience" to the lawfully imposed religion of the state. This means that "we so speak as, by lawful authority, we are commanded; and when we live accordingly; which, in sum, is trust and faith reposed in him that speaketh [the ruler], though the mind be incapable of any notion at all from the words spoken."[8] In a word, faith and obedience are what is essential to religion, not reason. Piety, not philosophy, is all that God expects of believers. There is complete separation of faith and fact. Hence, belief in objective factual miracles is not essential to true religious faith.

Immanuel Kant: Miracles Are Incompatible with True Religion

In many ways Kant (1724–1804) stands at the crossroad of modern philosophy. He not only synthesizes rationalism and empiricism but provides impetus to agnosticism and deism.

4. Ibid., pp. 82–83.
5. Ibid., p. 83.
6. Ibid., p. 70.
7. Ibid., pp. 70–71.
8. Ibid., p. 165.

Kant's impact on the history of philosophy has been felt especially in the area of epistemology. In one sense, Kant's view of miracles is far more helpful to naturalism than is Hume's. Hume's attack on supernaturalism is frontal but Kant's is subterranean.

Like Spinoza before him, Kant views morality as the heart of true religion, although their justification of this conclusion differs. According to Kant, "theoretical reason can never reach God."[9] There is a gulf that cannot be spanned between the world to us (*phenomena*) and the world in itself (*noumena*). We can know appearance but not reality. God can be known only by practical reason.[10] In fact, we must strive to live "within the limits of [practical] reason alone."[11] Foreshadowing Schleiermacher, Kant claims that we must use practical or moral reason to determine what is essential to religion. This moral reason should be a guide to interpreting the Bible. He even admits that "frequently this interpretation may, in the light of the text (of the revelation), appear forced—it may often really be forced; and yet if the text can possibly support it, it must be preferred to a literal interpretation."[12] In fact, the Bible's moral teaching cannot but convince us of its divine nature.[13] In this moral law, then, is the essence of true religion, the Spirit of God.[14]

Using morality as the rule for religious truth, Kant asserts that miracles are merely an appropriate introduction to Christianity but not strictly necessary for it. In fact, he says, moral religion must "in the end render superfluous the belief in miracles in general." To believe that miracles can be helpful to morality is really "senseless conceit."[15]

Kant admits that the life of Christ may be "nothing but miracles," but warns that in the use of these accounts "we do not make it a tenet of religion that the knowing, believing, and professing of them are themselves means whereby we can render ourselves well-pleasing to God."[16] By this he implies that it is not at all essential to the Christian faith to believe in miracles.

9. Kant, *Critique of Pure Reason.*
10. Immanuel Kant, *Critique of Practical Reason Alone* (New York: Bobbs-Merrill, 1956).
11. Kant, *Religion Within the Limits of Reason Alone.*
12. Ibid., pp. 100–101.
13. Ibid., p. 104.
14. Ibid., pp. 98, 103.
15. Ibid.
16. Ibid., pp. 79–80.

The very nature of a miracle is unknown to us. "We cannot know anything at all about supernatural aid."[17] One thing of which we can be sure is this: if an alleged miracle "flatly contradicts morality, it cannot, despite all appearances, be of God (for example, were a father ordered to kill his son who is, so far as he knows, perfectly innocent)."[18] Thus Kant uses the moral law to eliminate the Abraham–Isaac story in the Old Testament (Gen. 22).

Kant carries this moral argument against miracles even further. He insists that moral reason demands that we adopt the conclusion that miracles never happen.

> Those whose judgment in these matters is so inclined that they suppose themselves to be helpless without miracles, believe that they soften the blow which reason suffers from them by holding that they happen but seldom. [But we can ask] How seldom? Once in a hundred years? . . . Here we can determine nothing on the basis of knowledge of the object . . . but only on the basis of the maxims which are necessary for the use of our reason. Thus, miracles must be admitted as [occurring] daily (though indeed hidden under the guise of natural events) or else never. . . . Since the former alternative [that they occur daily] is not at all compatible with reason, nothing remains but to adopt the latter maxim—for this principle remains ever a mere maxim for making judgments, not a theoretical assertion. [For example, with regard to the] admirable conservation of the species in the plant and animal kingdoms, . . . no one, indeed, can claim to comprehend whether or not the direct influence of the Creator is required on each occasion. [Kant insists] they are for us, . . . nothing but natural effects and ought never to be adjudged otherwise. . . . To venture beyond these limits is rashness and immodesty.[19]

In brief, those who live by moral reason do not incorporate belief in miracles into their maxims (either of theoretical or practical reason) although they do not impugn their possibility or reality.[20] So, miracles may be possible, but it is never rational to believe in them, since reason is always based on universal laws.

In view of Kant's moral naturalism, it is not surprising that he rejects the account of the resurrection of Christ: "The more secret records, added as a sequel, of his resurrection and ascension . . . can-

17. Ibid., p. 79.
18. Ibid., p. 82.
19. Ibid., pp. 83–84.
20. Ibid., p. 83.

not be used in the interest of religion within the limits of reason alone without doing violence to their historical valuation."[21]

It is difficult to follow Kant's argument, because he implies but does not elaborate a crucial premise. But in view of what he taught elsewhere, the argument can be summarized as follows:

1. We cannot know the real world (the world in itself) by theoretical reason.
2. Everything in our experience (the world to us) must be determined by practical reason.
3. Practical reason operates according to universal laws.
4. Miracles must occur either daily, seldom, or never.
5. But what occurs daily is not a miracle; it occurs according to natural laws.
6. And what occurs seldom is not determined by any law.
7. But everything must be determined by practical reason that operates on universal laws (2 and 3).
8. Therefore, it is rationally necessary to conclude that miracles never occur.

In support of the crucial third premise, Kant notes that "In the affairs of life, therefore, it is impossible for us to count on miracles or to take them into consideration at all in our use of reason (and reason must be used in every incident of life)."[22] In short, miracles are theoretically possible but practically impossible. That is to say, we must live as if they never occur. If we live otherwise, then we overthrow the whole dictates of practical reason and the moral law, which is the essence of true religion. Therefore, admitting miracles occur and living in their light is not only unnecessary to religion, it is actually harmful to it. So, even if there are supernatural acts, we must live (and think) as if there are none. In short, even if God exists we should live like naturalists!

An Evaluation

Hobbes' statements on miracles do not demand refutation, since he offers no real argument but merely makes assertions. First, it is certainly true that we should not accept contradictions as true or mere "opinions

21. Ibid., p. 119.
22. Ibid., p. 82.

about ghosts." Second, as Hobbes points out, mere ignorance of a natural cause does not give us the right to conclude that there was a supernatural cause. Finally, it is sometimes true that faith in the sensational fades when things return to the ordinary. Certainly the purpose of miracles should not be to engender a dependence on the miraculous.

According to the biblical record, however, the purpose of miracles was to encourage dependence on God. The apostle John writes, "Jesus did many other miraculous signs [miracles] . . . but these are

is the Christ, the Son of
brews speaks of miracles as
his mouthpieces: "This sal-
who heard him. God also
is miracles" (Heb. 2:3–4).
epends on the audience's
was to confirm confidence
sperson was from God.
argument. We will note

osticism, which is implied
dical disjunction between
the world of our experi-
nconsistent with this sepa-
into the noumenal (real)
could do this consistently
nnot consistently separate
of both. A line cannot be
hort, to say "I know that
to know something about
ting.
egs the question by laying
ase, the rule is rational; in
e, it is methodological; in
there is some interpretive
ds a uniformitarian under-
demands regulating all of
ason). And since he allows

no exceptions to a law, there are no exceptions to the rule that says, "Live as if there are no miracles."

But this begs the question. Why should we assume there are no exceptions to any laws? Or, to put it another way, why should we assume that everything comes under some law? Maybe there are some singularities, like the origin of the world or history of the earth, that defy any classification with other events.

Third, Kant believed, as did others of his day, that Newton's law of gravitation was universally true, with no exceptions. This "Newtonian" view of law as universal and absolutely determinable is no longer held by modern scientists. Natural law is now thought of as general and statistical, but not necessarily universal and without exceptions. With this view, the problem of admitting unrepeatable exceptions (which miracles would be) is resolved. But if Kant is wrong in his view of scientific law—insisting that every event be subsumed under some natural law—then his moral objection to miracles fails.

Finally, Kant's approach to the Gospel is not historical but moral. Rather than looking at the historical evidence for an event (like the resurrection), he summarily dismisses it as unauthentic because it is morally unessential. Kant admits that this moral hermeneutic will often be "forced," but he insists that it must be accepted rather than the "literal" understanding. Why? Not because the historical facts support it, but simply because his understanding of the moral law demands it. In short, historical truth is determined a priori (by moral law), not a posteriori from the facts. History is determined by morality, what is (or was) through what ought to be.

If Kant's argument is correct, then we should live as if miracles do not occur—even if some have occurred! This leads to the astounding conclusion that we should order our life by a form of (practical) reason even if it is contrary to fact. Surely Freud would have called this an illusion. At any rate, if a miracle actually happened, Kant would insist we live according to "reason," which says we live as if miracles do not happen. But this amounts to saying that we should "reason" in practice that what is true is false! But this is an unreasonable use of reason.

It would appear that the attempt to show that miracles are not essential to Christianity on religious or moral grounds fails. Hobbes commends (probably with tongue in cheek) blind religious faith in the supernatural, even when it contradicts reason. Along with this fideism, he satirically reminds us that miracles do not really help faith anyway. This, however, is not necessarily true, at least not if the purpose of miracles is to encourage and confirm faith in God and not just to engender reliance on the sensational.

Kant's attack on miracles is more fundamental. He sees them not only as unessential but fundamentally unnecessary to the essence of true religion which he takes to mean living in accordance with the universal dictates of practical reason. Besides Kant's self-defeating agnosticism, he begs the question both by assuming a moral uniformitarianism and by misunderstanding the nature of scientific "law" as universally applicable, rather than as a statistical generalization. In fact, in order for Kant to avoid the miraculous, he is forced to engage in an attempt to interpret the basic documents of Christianity by eliminating the miracle accounts without any historical reason for doing so.

Whether miracles be true or false, for better or for worse, historic Christianity claims they are an essential part of its beliefs. Christianity without miracles is Christianity without Christ, since his life was one long miracle from start to finish. So it makes a significant difference to the truth of Christianity (and its survival) as to whether miracles are essential to its belief. And whatever else may be said for Kant's attempt to show that miracles are not essential to religion in general, it certainly does not apply to Christianity in particular.

 **9**

ARE MIRACLES DEFINABLE?

Each miracle writes for us in small letters something that God
has already written, in letters almost too large to be noticed,
across the whole canvas of Nature.—C. S. Lewis

IN THE PREVIOUS CHAPTERS we have examined the most significant
arguments against miracles from the seventeenth century to the present. We concluded that in varying ways each naturalist pressed his
case unsuccessfully. None succeeded in eliminating the possibility of
miracles. One thing that did emerge, however, was the need to identify a miracle before one could be known to have occurred. That is,
granted that miracles are identifiable in terms of some supernatural
source (God), some specific distinguishing characteristics of miracles
must be delineated before we can point to a given event as one that
possesses these characteristics. Simply to say it is a singularity is insuf-
ficient. There are some singularities that are not supernaturally caused.

The question of the definition of miracles, then, is still prelimi-
nary to the actual identification of a miracle. (Whether such an identification can be successfully made will be the subject of chap. 11.)
Since the biblical claim for miracles is at the center of the contro-
versy, we turn now to a discussion and definition of the miracles
described in the Bible.

A Biblical Description of Miracles

The Bible uses three basic words to describe a miracle: sign, wonder, and power.

93

The Old Testament

Although the Hebrew word for sign (*'ôt*) is sometimes used to refer to natural things such as stars (Gen. 1:14) or the sabbath (Exod. 31:13), it is most often used to refer to something appointed by God with special assigned meaning.

The first usage of the word "sign" is in the divine prediction given to Moses that Israel will be delivered from Egypt and serve God at Horeb. God says, "I will be with you. And this will be the sign to you that it is I who have sent you" (Exod. 3:12). When Moses asks God, "What if they do not believe me or listen to me?" the Lord gives Moses two "signs": his rod turns into a snake (Exod. 4:3) and his hand becomes leprous (Exod. 4:1–7). These are given "that they may believe that the LORD, the God of their fathers . . . has appeared to you" (Exod. 4:5). God says, "If they do not believe you or pay attention to the first miraculous sign, they may believe the second" (Exod. 4:8). Moses "performed the signs before the people, and they believed; . . . they bowed down and worshiped" (Exod. 4:30–31). In fact, God says, "I will harden [strengthen] Pharaoh's heart, and though I multiply my miraculous signs and wonders in Egypt, he will not listen to you. . . . And the Egyptians will know that I am the LORD when I stretch out my hand against Egypt and bring the Israelites out of it" (Exod. 7:3, 5; cf. 11:9).

Again and again it is repeated that the purpose of these signs is twofold: "By this you will know that I am the LORD" (Exod. 7:17; 9:29–30; 10:1–2) and that these are "my people" (Exod. 3:10; 5:1; 6:7; 11:7). The more the Lord multiplies the signs, the harder Pharaoh's heart becomes (Exod. 7:3, 5; cf. 11:9). But even through stubborn unbelief God receives "glory" (Num. 14:22).

Throughout the rest of the Old Testament there are repeated references to the miraculous "signs" God performed in delivering his people from Egypt. God complains to Moses in the wilderness: "How long will they refuse to believe in me, in spite of all the miraculous signs I have performed among them?" (Num. 14:11; cf. v. 22). Moses challenges Israel: "Has any god ever tried to take for himself one nation out of another nation, by testings, by miraculous signs and wonders?" (Deut. 4:34). Later Moses reminds the people, "The LORD sent miraculous signs and wonders—great and terrible—upon Egypt and Pharaoh and his whole household" (Deut. 6:22). "The LORD brought us out of Egypt with a mighty hand and an outstretched arm, with great terror and with miraculous signs and wonders" (Deut. 26:8; cf. 29:2–3; Josh. 24:17; Neh. 9:10; Ps. 105:27; Jer. 32:20–21).

Many times in the biblical record "signs" are given to prophets as confirmation of their divine call. Moses' miraculous credentials have already been mentioned. Gideon asks of God, "Give me a sign that it is really you talking with me" (Judg. 6:17). God responds with miraculous fire that consumes Gideon's offering (v. 21). God confirms himself to Eli by miraculous predictions about his sons' deaths (1 Sam. 2:34). Likewise, predictive "signs" are made to confirm God's appointment of Saul as king (1 Sam. 10:7, 9). Isaiah offers predictions as "signs" of his divine message (Isa. 7:14; 38:22). Although the word "sign" is not used in these cases, God's miraculous confirmation of Moses over Korah (Num. 16) and Elijah over the false prophets of Baal (1 Kings 18) illustrate the same point. In short, miracles are signs accrediting the true prophet. Likewise, the lack of predictive powers (false prophecies) is an indication that the prophet is not of God (Deut. 18:22).

Other events in the Old Testament are called "signs" or miracles as well. These include the plagues on Egypt (Exod. 7:3), the provisions in the wilderness (John 6:30–31), fire from a rock (Judg. 6:17–21), victory over enemies (1 Sam. 14:10), confirmation of healing (Isa. 38:7, 22), and judgments from the Lord (Jer. 44:29).

Often the words "sign" and "wonder" are used of the same event(s) in the same verse (Exod. 7:3; Deut. 4:34; 7:19; 13:1–2; 26:8; 28:46; 29:3; 34:11; Neh. 9:10; Ps. 135:9; Jer. 32:20–21). At other times the Bible describes as "wonders" the same events that are elsewhere called "signs" (Exod. 4:21; 11:9–10; Pss. 78:43; 105:27; Joel 2:30). Of course, sometimes the word is used of a natural "wonder," as of a prophet (Ezek. 24:24) or a unique thing a prophet does to get God's message across (Isa. 20:3). But even here the word "wonder" has a special supernatural (divine) significance.

One Hebrew word for "power" (*kōaḥ*) is sometimes used of human power in the Old Testament (Gen. 31:6; Deut. 8:17; Nah. 2:1). But very often it is used of divine power. Sometimes it is used of God's power to create: "God made the earth by his power . . . and stretched out the heavens by his understanding" (Jer. 10:12; see also Jer. 27:5; 32:17; 51:15). In other places the "power" of God overthrows his enemies (Exod. 15:6–7), delivers his people from Egypt (Num. 14:17; cf. v. 13), rules the universe (1 Chron. 29:12), gives Israel their land (Ps. 111:6), and inspires his prophets to speak his Word (Mic. 3:8). "Power" is often used in direct connection with events called "signs" or "wonders" or both (see Exod. 9:16; 32:11; Deut. 4:37; 2 Kings 17:36; Neh. 1:10). Sometimes other Hebrew words for power are used in the same verse with "signs and wonders." Moses speaks of the deliverance of Israel "by miraculous signs and wonders . . . and by a mighty hand" (Deut. 4:34; cf. 7:19; 26:8; 34:12).

The New Testament

The New Testament usage of the three basic words for miracles is directly parallel to that of the Old Testament.

In the New Testament, sign (*sēmeion*) is used seventy-seven times (forty-eight times in the Gospels). It is occasionally used of ordinary events, such as circumcision (Rom. 4:11), and of a baby wrapped in swaddling clothes (Luke 2:12). Here again these signs have special divine significance. Most often the word is reserved for what we would call a miracle. Many times it is used of Jesus' miracles, such as healing (John 6:2; 9:16), turning the water to wine (John 2:11), and raising the dead (John 11:47). Likewise, the apostles did miracles of healing (Acts 4:16, 30), "great signs and miracles" (Acts 8:13), and "miraculous signs and wonders" (Acts 14:3; 15:12); "many wonders and miraculous signs were done by the apostles" (Acts 2:43). Even the Jewish authorities said, "What are we going to do with these men? Everyone living in Jerusalem knows they have done an outstanding miracle, and we cannot deny it" (Acts 4:16).

The word "sign" is also used of the most significant miracle in the New Testament, the resurrection of Jesus Christ from the grave. Jesus said to his unbelieving generation, The "Son of Man will be three days and three nights in the heart of the earth" (Matt. 12:39–40). Jesus repeated this prediction of his resurrection when he was asked for a sign (Matt. 16:1, 4). Not only was the resurrection a miracle, but it was a miracle that Jesus predicted (Matt. 12:40; 16:21; 20:19; John 2:19).

The word "wonder" (*teras*) is used sixteen times in the New Testament and almost always refers to a miracle.[1] In fact, in every occurrence it is used in combination with the word "sign." It is used of the supernatural events before the second coming of Christ (Matt. 24:24; Mark 13:22; Acts 2:19), of Jesus' miracles (John 4:48; Acts 2:22), of the apostles' miracles (Acts 2:43; cf. Acts 4:30; 5:12; Heb.

---

1. The word is used once of a satanic sign in 2 Thess. 2:9, but is qualified as a "lying" sign and wonder.

2:3–4), of Stephen's miracles (Acts 6:8), of Moses' miracles in Egypt (Acts 7:36), and of Paul's miracles (Acts 14:3; 15:12; Rom. 15:19). The Greek word *teras* means a "miraculous sign, prodigy, portent, omen, wonder." It carries with it the idea of that which is amazing or astonishing.[2]

The word "power" (*dunamis*) is used on numerous occasions in the New Testament. It is occasionally used of human power (2 Cor. 1:8) or abilities (Matt. 25:15). Sometimes it is used of spiritual (satanic) powers (Luke 10:19; Rom. 8:38). Like its Old Testament parallel, the New Testament term "power" is often translated "miracles." *Dunamis* is used in combination with signs and wonders (Heb. 2:4), of Christ's miracles (Matt. 13:58), of the power to raise the dead (Phil. 3:10), of the virgin birth of Christ (Luke 1:35), of the special gift of miracles (1 Cor. 12:10), of the outpouring of the Holy Spirit at Pentecost (Acts 1:8), and of the "power" of the gospel to save sinful people (Rom. 1:16). The emphasis of the word is on the divine energizing aspect of a miraculous event.

The Purposes of Miracles in the Bible

In the Old Testament miracle-working power was given as divine confirmation of a prophet or spokesperson for God. When Moses protested to God that Israel would not believe him, God replied by giving him the ability to turn his rod into a snake in order "that they may believe that the LORD, the God of their fathers . . . has appeared to you" (Exod. 4:1–5). Likewise, when Korah challenged Moses' divine authority, God confirmed his servant Moses by opening up the earth to swallow Korah (Num. 16). When Israel hesitated between the god Baal and Yahweh, God confirmed Elijah over the prophets of Baal by sending fire from heaven to consume the sacrifices, praying, "let it be known today that you are God in Israel and that I am your servant" (1 Kings 18:36).

Miracles in the New Testament also have a confirmatory purpose. John said, "This, the first of his miraculous signs, Jesus performed in Cana of Galilee. He thus revealed his glory, and his disciples put their faith in him" (John 2:11); "Jesus did many other miraculous signs . . . but these are written that you may believe that Jesus is the Christ" (John 20:30–31).

---

2. Colin Brown, ed., *Dictionary of New Testament Theology* (Grand Rapids: Zondervan, 1976), 2:633, 623–25. See the parallel word for "wonder" (*thauma*).

Another purpose of miraculous "signs" is as a divine confirmation
of a prophet of God. The religious ruler Nicodemus said of Jesus:
"We know you are a teacher who has come from God. For no one
could perform the miraculous signs you are doing if God were not
with him" (John 3:2). Many people followed him, because they saw
the signs he performed on those who were sick (John 6:2). When
some rejected Jesus, even though he had cured a blind man, others
said, "How can a sinner do such miraculous signs?" (John 9:16).
The apostles were confident in proclaiming, "Jesus the Nazarene was
a man accredited by God to you by miracles, wonders and signs,
which God did among you through him, as you yourselves know"
(Acts 2:22). For his credentials to the Corinthians, the apostle Paul
claimed that the signs of a true apostle were performed among them
(2 Cor. 12:12). He and Barnabas recounted to the apostles "the
miraculous signs and wonders God had done among the Gentiles
through them" (Acts 15:12).

Perhaps the most definitive passage on miracles in the New
Testament is Hebrews 2:3–4. "How shall we escape if we neglect so
great a salvation? After it was at the first spoken through the Lord, it
was confirmed to us by those [apostles] who heard, God also bearing
witness with them, both by signs and wonders and by various miracles." In short, miracles are God's way of accrediting his spokesper-
sons. There is a miracle to confirm the message as true, a sign to sub-
stantiate the sermon, an act of God to verify the Word of God.

The Definition of a Miracle

Now that we have the essential biblical data in front of us, we are
in a position to define miracles. A miracle, of course, is a special act
of God in the natural world, something nature would not have done
on its own (see chap. 1). The three words Scripture uses to describe
a miracle help us to delineate that meaning more precisely.

Each of the three words for supernatural events (sign, wonder,
power) delineates an aspect of a miracle. The biblical concept of
"miracle" stands in contrast to "nature." Nature is the usual, regular
pattern of God's activity. As such, it can be predicted and, in this
sense, "controlled" by people for their own use and benefit. Nature
is the domain over which God gave humankind dominion (Gen.
1:28).

From the human vantage point a miracle, then, is an unusual
event ("wonder") that conveys and confirms an unusual message

("sign") by means of unusual power ("power"). From the divine vantage point a miracle is an act of God ("power") that attracts the attention of the people of God ("wonder") to the Word of God (by a "sign").

According to the Bible, a miracle has several dimensions. First, it has an unusual character. It is an out-of-the-ordinary event in contrast to the regular pattern of events in the natural world. It is a "wonder" that attracts attention by its uniqueness. A burning bush that is not consumed, fire from heaven, and walking on water are not normal occurrences. Hence, they will by their unusual character draw the interest of observers.

Second, there is a theological dimension. A miracle is an act of God. Hence, it presupposes that there is a God who can act. The view that there is a God beyond the universe who created it, controls it, and can interfere in it is called theism. Miracles, then, imply a theistic view of the universe.

Third, miracles have a moral dimension. They bring glory to God. That is, they manifest the moral character of God. Miracles are visible acts that reflect the invisible nature of God. Technically, there are no evil miracles, then, because God is good. All miracles by nature aim to produce and/or promote good.

Fourth, miracles have a doctrinal dimension. Miracles in the Bible are connected directly or indirectly with "truth claims." They are ways to tell a true prophet from a false prophet (Deut. 18:22). They confirm the truth of God through the servant of God (Heb. 2:3–4). A miracle is the sign that confirms the sermon. Message and miracle go hand-in-hand.

Fifth, biblical miracles have a teleological dimension. Unlike magic, they are never performed to entertain (see Luke 23:8). Miracles have a distinctive purpose: to glorify the Creator and to provide evidence for people to believe by accrediting the message of God through the prophet of God.

The Context of Miracles

An essential feature of biblical miracles is their theistic context. This means that a person must be operating within a theistic worldview in order to identify a miracle. To illustrate, let us consider a few incidents in the life of Moses. Initially, when Moses came upon the burning bush (Exod. 3:1–6), he began to investigate it because of its unusual nature. The accompanying word from God reveals that

Moses was not just in the presence of an unusual event but of a miracle. Because Moses operated within a theistic framework, he had sufficient basis to judge the event to be a miracle.

If Moses had reported to convinced atheists what had happened (how God had spoken to him out of a burning bush), they would have been within their rights to doubt the story. Since in an atheistic universe there is no God, it makes no sense to them to speak about acts of a God who does not exist. Without a theistic context, a burning bush and a voice may seem no more miraculous than the voice from heaven did to those who took it as thunder (John 12:29). But granting God exists and we know something about his rational and moral nature, these defining characteristics of a miracle can help us identify one when it occurs.

# 10

ARE MIRACLES ANTINATURAL?

> God does not shake miracles into Nature at random as if from
> a pepper-caster.—C. S. Lewis

INNUMERABLE IMPLAUSIBLE EVENTS believed by some to be miracles
are alleged to have occurred. But to the modern mind these events
appear to be incredible. One of the underlying and residual obstacles regarding miracles, for modern thinkers, is that they seem so
unnatural as to be antinatural.

Miracle Stories

During the second and third centuries numerous books written
by various religious groups related bizarre stories about the childhood of Christ. Take, for example, the miracle story from the apocryphal book, *The Protoevangelium of James:*

> I looked up at the vault of heaven, and saw it standing still and the birds
> of the heaven motionless. And I looked at the earth, and saw a dish
> placed there and workmen lying round it, with their hands in the dish.
> But those who chewed did not chew, and those who lifted up anything
> lifted up nothing. . . . And behold, sheep were being driven and (yet)
> they did not come forward, but stood still. . . . And I looked at the flow
> of the river, and saw the mouths of the kids over it and they did not
> drink. And then all at once everything went on its course (again).[1]

1. *The Protoevangelium of James* 18.2. Unless otherwise indicated, all references
to the apocryphal books are from the *New Testament Apocrypha*, ed. Edgar Henneck,
2 vols. (Philadelphia: Westminster, 1963).

The child Jesus is said to have performed some highly odd feats. As a five-year-old boy playing in the brook, he made soft clay and fashioned from it twelve sparrows. . . . Jesus clapped his hands and cried to the sparrows: "Off with you!" And the sparrows took flight and went away chirping. [The story continues.] But the son of Annas the scribe was standing there with Joseph; and he took a branch of a willow and (with it) dispersed the water which Jesus had gathered together. When Jesus saw what he had done he was enraged and said to him: "You insolent, godless dunderhead, what harm did the pools and the water do to you?" [Forthwith Jesus cursed him] and immediately that lad withered up completely.[2]

When Jesus was blamed for the death of a neighbor boy, "immediately those who had accused him became blind."[3] This is strikingly odd in comparison to the miracles in the Gospels, all of which demonstrate that Jesus had a positive effect on human beings.[4]

Medieval accounts of miracles are nothing less than incredible. Paul Sabatier, in his *Life of Francis of Assisi,* cites a number of odd miracle stories. "In one case a parrot being carried away by a kite uttered the invocation dear to his master, '*Sancte Thoma, adjuva me*' [Saint Thomas, save me] and was immediately rescued." In another case, "A merchant of Groningen, having purloined an arm of St. John the Baptist, grew rich as if by enchantment, so long as he kept it concealed in his house, but was reduced to beggary so soon as . . . the relic was taken away from him and placed in a church."[5]

Some stories of religious relic miracles are also bizarre. "Bernard of Clairvaux, for example, when in extremities, needed to be saved from without—by the intervention of Mary, who gave him her breast."[6] In one case "a cleric in his illness had bitten off his tongue and lips, and was suddenly healed by Mary's milk." When the healing power of the milk was observed, it was "gathered up and saved as a relic."[7]

Other reported medieval miracles include the "stigmata" or bleeding wounds of a living saint in emulation of Jesus' wounds[8] and

2. *Infancy Story of Thomas* 2.1–4; 3.1–3.
3. Ibid., 5.1.
4. The only negative miracle in the Gospels is the withered fig tree (Matt. 21:18–22).
5. As quoted by B. B. Warfield, *Counterfeit Miracles* (New York: Scribner, 1918), pp. 66–67.
6. Ibid., p. 251.
7. Ibid., p. 269.
8. Ibid., p. 262.

St. Anne's wrist bone, which is called the "Great Relic" and was venerated by thousands of people, reportedly resulting in some healings.[9] Strangely, even some modern Roman Catholic scholars defend both of these kinds of "miracles" and the veneration of relics.[10]

The ancients hold no monopoly on bizarre miracle stories, however. From time to time there are reports of icons shedding tears or bleeding. The most unusual stories, however, are not limited to Catholic saints. I once witnessed the son of a Protestant minister who claimed to be able to see without an eye. David Pelliter had lost his left eye because of an accident. He and his father claimed his vision was later restored as the result of prayer. Along with several hundred graduate students and professors, I personally saw him take out his glass eye, cover the other one, and read things collected at random from the audience. I was not only convinced at the time it was a modern miracle but spoke of it publicly many times for years.[11]

This unusual occurrence was odd by comparison to biblical miracles. First, while Jesus healed withered hands, there is no record that he ever created one that was maimed. Jesus healed blindness but never caused anyone to see physical objects without a physical eye. There is something unnatural, if not antinatural, about seeing without an eye. Restoring a natural function befits the Creator of nature, but seeing without an eye bypasses (if not negates) the natural power God created.

These accounts of purported miracles are not really *super*natural; rather, they are *anti*natural. How, for example, can the whole course of nature freeze for a few moments and then resume? Even if it were possible, what possible use would a rational God have for such an incredibly bizarre occurrence? The miracles of the Bible, although unusual and obviously divine in their origin, clearly demonstrate the character of God. They evidence purpose and order, something the more ridiculous miracle stories do not. Even some of the alleged childhood miracles of Jesus do not really fit into the natural world. Indeed, most of these apocryphal miracles are very unlike the miracles of the Bible.

9. Ibid., p. 274.

10. Jacques Douillet, *What Is a Saint?* (New York: Hawthorne, 1958), pp. 63, 100.

11. Only after further research was I convinced that those who purportedly see without an eye are merely using a skilled magical trick to deceive the audience. No matter how good a blindfold may seem to be, there is an opening along the bridge of the nose through which a person can see.

As C. S. Lewis notes, "If we open such books as Grimm's *Fairy Tales* or Ovid's *Metamorphoses* or the Italian epics we find ourselves in a world of miracles so diverse that they can hardly be classified." In them "beasts turn into men and men into beasts or trees, trees talk, ships become goddesses, and a magic ring can cause tables richly spread with food to appear in solitary places." If such things really happened, they would "show that Nature was being invaded. But they would show that she was being invaded by an alien power."[12] These fantasies, like many early and medieval Christian miracles, do not really fit into nature. Indeed, some early and medieval miracle stories bear a much stronger resemblance to fantasy stories than to the biblical records of miracles. Most are in fact antinatural.

Biblical Miracles Are Not Antinatural

Biblical miracles stand in strong contrast to these apocryphal miracle stories and fairy tales. While theists sometimes describe miracles as "contrary to nature," they do not mean *against* nature but rather *beyond* it. They mean miracles are contrary to the way things *normally* work, not contrary to the way things *actually* are. When a miracle occurs nature is not disrupted from its regular patterns. In fact, like a stick cast into the river, once a miracle occurs it is absorbed into the flow of natural law. For example, the blind eyes Jesus supernaturally restored saw in a natural way. The legs he restored walked in a natural way. A miracle interjects something new into nature that nature would not have produced, but once it is produced it is absorbed into the natural rhythm of the physical universe. So, the miracles of the New Testament are not antinatural. "The fitness of the Christian miracles," notes Lewis, "and their difference from these mythological miracles, lies in the fact that they show invasion by a Power which is not alien." They are, in fact, "what might be expected to happen when she is invaded not simply by a god, but by the God of Nature: by a Power which is outside her jurisdiction not as a foreigner but as a sovereign."[13]

For example, the miracles of the Old Testament are not contrary to nature. Some Old Testament miracles are healings that restore the natural working of the physical body (2 Kings 5); some are raisings from the dead (2 Kings 4) or from near death (Jon. 2). Even when

---

12. C. S. Lewis, *Miracles* (New York: Macmillan, 1947), p. 132.
13. Ibid.

the miracles involve judgment on nature (Exod. 7–12; Num. 16:28–34) it is in view of its ultimate redemption (Isa. 65:25; 66:25). When the Red Sea is divided the natural force of wind is involved (Exod. 14:21). The manna from heaven comes with the night dew and spoils if kept too long (Exod. 16:11–15). All miracles fit into God's plan to redeem both his people and nature (Gen. 3:15; Rom. 8:18–25).

Jesus and the New Testament writers do not view Old Testament events as myths (cf. 1 Tim. 4:6–7; 2 Tim. 4:4; Titus 1:10–14). Jesus affirms the historicity of Adam and Eve (Matt. 19:4–5), Noah and the flood (Matt. 24:37–39), Jonah (Matt. 12:40), the serpent in the wilderness (John 3:14), Elijah's miracles (Luke 4:26), and numerous other events, most of which have miraculous elements.

The same is true in the New Testament. Jesus' healing ministry is one of restoring nature. Indeed, the whole process of redemption involves the restoration of the physical creation (Rom. 8) that has been marred by sin and death (Rom. 5).

Biblical miracles are not against nature; many are largely a speeding up of natural processes. "I contend," says Lewis, "that in all these [biblical] miracles alike the incarnate God does suddenly and locally something that God has done or will do in general." That is to say, "Each miracle writes for us in small letters something that God has already written, or will write, in letters almost too large to be noticed, across the whole canvas of Nature." Hence, "Not one of them is isolated or anomalous: each carries the signature of the God whom we know through conscience and from Nature. Their authenticity is attested by the style."[14]

The point here is simply, if God is the author of our (inward) moral nature and of (external) physical nature, we already know his "style" of working (cf. Acts 17:29; Rom. 1:19–20; 2:12–14). Therefore, so-called miracles that are against this style (antinatural) are judged unauthentic, and miracles in this style can be considered authentic. For God may wish to perfect the form of things he has made, but he does not work (even by miracles) against his work.

Of course, knowing God's "style" is not automatic, any more than is knowing the style of any great artist. It takes the training of our moral and theological faculties to recognize the moral and theological dimensions of a miracle. Jesus performed many miracles in the Gospels. The first of these was the conversion of water into wine

14. Ibid., p. 140.

(John 2). Other than the unusual suddenness of the event, this should not be surprising to anyone who is accustomed to God's way of working in natural processes. "In a certain sense, He constantly turns water into wine, for wine, like all drinks, is but water modified. Once, and in one year only, God, now incarnate, short circuits the process: makes wine in a moment. . . . The Miracle consists in the short cut; but the event to which it leads is the usual one."[15]

The miraculous feeding of thousands (Matt. 14:15–21; 15:32–38) falls into this same category. "They involve the multiplication of a little bread and a little fish into much bread and much fish." Again, this is not antinatural. For "every year God makes a little corn into much corn: the seed is sown and there is an increase."[16] The same pattern is seen in multiplied fish. "Look down into every bay and almost every river. This swarming, undulating fecundity shows He is still at work 'thronging the seas with spawn innumerable.' Thus, it is not contra-natural for Jesus to multiply fish. For it was God who at the beginning commanded all species 'to be fruitful and multiply and replenish the earth.' And now, that day, at the feeding of the thousands, incarnate God does the same; does close and small, under His human hands . . . what He has always been doing in the seas, the lakes and the little brooks."[17]

To some the virgin birth seems to be an antinatural way to be born. To be sure, it is unnatural, but it is not thereby against nature. After all, the virgin conception resulted in a normal nine-month pregnancy and a natural birth. Some consider Jesus' miraculous conception to be a slur on sexual intercourse. This, however, is no more true than feeding the five thousand is an insult to bakers.[18] Something about the event had to be highly unusual. Otherwise it would not qualify as a miracle. And having no male fertilization is highly unusual. This does not make the virgin birth of Christ antinatural, however, for two basic reasons.

First, as already noted, even the virgin conception resulted in a normal nine-month pregnancy and a natural childbirth. Furthermore, "if we believe that God created Nature that momentum [i.e., creation of life] comes from Him. The human father is merely an instrument, a carrier . . . simply the last in a long line of carriers—a line that stretches back far beyond his ancestors . . . back to the creation

15. Ibid., p. 141.
16. Ibid., p. 142.
17. Ibid.
18. Ibid.

of matter itself. That line is in God's hand. It is the instrument by which He normally creates a man."[19]

In short, ultimately God's creative powers are necessary in every birth, to say nothing of one by a virgin. The main difference, then, is not that one is natural and the other is of God. It is that one is a direct and the other an indirect use of God's creative power.

Jesus performed many healing miracles. This too is not against nature. In a real sense the doctor never heals anything; nature heals. More properly God heals through natural processes. For example, a doctor can set a broken bone, but it is God who makes it grow back together. Hence, other than the unusual speed by which Jesus healed, there is nothing essentially contrary to nature in a physical healing. After all, Jesus did not create special radar for the blind or produce bionic legs for the lame. He healed natural eyes and strengthened natural legs. Even the one so-called negative miracle that Jesus performed, cursing the fig tree so that it withered, is not antinatural. For that is precisely what fig trees ultimately do—wither and die. And even this "negative" miracle he did not perform without a positive purpose. For this miracle is an acted parable, a symbol of God's desire to see his people be fruitful. Of course, simply because these miracles are not contrary to nature does not make them purely natural. Their unusual and "divine" dimensions qualify them as supernatural.

Jesus raised people from the dead. Does not the natural human mortality render resurrection miracles as antinatural? Not really. It may be contrary to the usual, but it is not contrary to the natural desire to live on after death. Further, the reversal of death and decay is not against nature; it is in fact *for* nature's rejuvenation. As C. S. Lewis aptly puts it, "Entropy by its very character assures us that though it may be the universal rule in the Nature we know, it cannot be universal absolutely." For "a Nature which is 'running down' cannot be the whole story. A clock can't run down unless it has been wound up. . . . If a Nature which disintegrates order were the whole of reality, where would she find any order to disintegrate! Thus on any view there must have been time when processes the reverse of those we now see were going on: a time of winding up."[20]

And if it was once "natural" to generate life that is now degenerating, then it is not unnatural if it be regenerated (via resurrection).

19. Ibid., p. 143.
20. Ibid., p. 157.

Indeed, this is what is involved in the "grand miracle"[21] of the death and resurrection of Christ.

If resurrection is not against the natural, then the other miracles of the "new creation,"[22] such as Christ's transfiguration, walking on water, and otherwise dominating nature, may just be foretastes or "firstfruits" (1 Cor. 15:20) of the new nature to come (Rev. 21:1–5). This domination of nature by the Spirit is by no means contra-natural. For the "Spirit by dominating Nature confirms and improves natural activities. The brain does not become less a brain by being used for rational thought."[23]

Miracle and Nature

Let us now summarize the similarities and differences between a miracle and a natural process. First of all, both have the same source—God. Neither nature nor miracle is self-caused. Both find their root in the supernatural. Nature is the result of the first great miracle—creation. A miracle involves a similar but smaller creative intervention of God. It is an event in the natural world that would not have happened were nature left to itself.[24]

Second, a miracle is physically similar to nature. It is similar to the natural process. Many miracles involve a speeding up of a natural process. They are a shortcut to what nature does regularly. They are a microcosm of the macrocosm of nature. Other miracles improve nature and anticipate its regeneration (resurrection). In fact, nature itself rehearses annually and seasonally its own regeneration with autumn (death) and spring (life). In this sense all miracles fit into the natural world and natural expectations.

Third, there is a moral similarity between miracles and nature. Miracles—acts of God—are like God. They are in accord with the natural moral law of God (Rom. 2:12–15). No miracles have evil or destructive purposes, even those that involve just punishment. Rather, their purposes are good; they are in accord with the natural

21. Ibid., pp. 112ff.
22. Lewis articulates two broad categories of miracles: (1) miracles of the "old creation" that basically accelerate nature; and (2) miracles of the "new creation" that regenerate nature or what nature will be like after Christ's return.
23. Ibid., p. 132.
24. Some supernaturalists would say that a miracle is what nature "could not" (not just "would not") do on its own without intelligent (divine) intervention.

law of God. So then miracles have a good purpose and goal—the ultimate deliverance of the natural world (Rom. 8:19–21).

Fourth, nature and miracles differ in their regularity and predictability. Nature operates in regular and predictable patterns, and it is thus under our control (Gen. 1:28). Miracles are by nature irregular and unpredictable and, hence, are not under our control. But even here the origin of the natural world is an unrepeatable singular event, as is a miracle.

In short, genuine miracles come from beyond nature; they befit nature and they benefit nature. Their source is God; their nature is God-like, and their goal is good. Counterfeit "miracles" lack these characteristics and some are even antinatural.

Throughout both pagan and Christian history many bizarre events have been labeled miraculous. Many of these events do not fit into nature, and some are even contrary to nature. Hence, they do not have the required theistic context to qualify as miracles. They have neither the divine context nor the divine style.

Biblical miracles not only fit into nature but even perfect nature. Biblical miracles are not antinatural; they are simply unnatural. That is, they are not contranatural, but supernatural. They are not against nature but come from beyond nature. They are not unlike nature, however, for nature resembles its Creator (see Ps. 19:1–4). Many biblical miracles involve a speeding up of natural processes. All fit into nature. Some anticipate the renewal and regeneration of nature but never its ultimate destruction. Just as a nature that is "running down" was once "wound up," so resurrection and new creation miracles signal the "rewinding" or regeneration of nature. In this regard, biblical miracles are far from against nature. They are for nature by coming from beyond it and by working to perfect what is within it.

 **11**

ARE MIRACLES DISTINGUISHABLE?

Their authenticity is attested by their style.—C. S. Lewis

THE WORD "MIRACLE" has a broad usage in our culture. In general the word is used to describe almost anything that is unusual. But not all unusual events are supernatural. Thus, it is necessary to distinguish several kinds of unusual events that are sometimes confused with miracles.

Natural Events

Some natural events are unusual (anomalies) but are still natural events. A natural event happens in accord with natural law, even if it does not occur at identical intervals (e.g., meteors falling to earth).

Natural law is a description of the way God acts regularly in and through creation (Ps. 104:10–14), whereas a miracle is the way God acts on special occasions. So both miracles and natural law involve the activity of God. The difference is that natural law is the regular, repeatable, and predictable way God acts, whereas a miracle is not.

Natural law is the way God acts indirectly in and through the world he has made. By contrast, a miracle is the way God acts directly in his creation from time to time.

Natural law describes the gradual activity of God in the world, whereas miracles manifest his immediate actions. In this sense, although there is more to it, a miracle is sometimes a speeding up of a natural process. For example, water turns into wine naturally (grad-

111

ually) as the rain goes in the soil, up the vine, and into the grape. It was a miracle, however, when Jesus did this immediately (John 2).

All usual events are natural, but not all unusual events are supernatural. Failing to take note of this, overzealous believers have sometimes mistaken anomalies of nature for supernatural interventions in nature. To the everlasting embarrassment of pre-Darwinian creationists, they sometimes identified earthquakes, tornadoes, meteors, and eclipses as supernatural—all because they had no natural explanation for them. This proved to be a fatal flaw in their thinking. For, as later natural explanations were found for these events, it tended to discredit supernaturalism in general. This was an unfortunate turn of events for credible supernaturalism, since confidence gained from overthrowing previously naturalistic interpretations of purely natural events tended to support the antisupernaturalist's claim that all unusual events would eventually yield to a naturalistic explanation.[1]

How, then, can a miracle be distinguished from an anomaly? One tell-tale characteristic of a natural event is the regularity of the series of events. If an event occurs regularly, no matter how unusual it is, then it is a natural event. Miracles, on the other hand, are not regular events. If they were, they would not be miracles. For example, it is unusual for physical objects to contract as they get colder, as water does when it reaches 32° Fahrenheit. However, it does this regularly. Hence, it is not a miracle. It is a natural event and has a natural cause.

Simply because we do not have an explanation for an unusual event does not mean it is miraculous. For example, scientists have not yet discovered how life grows on thermo-vents in the depth of the seas, but it does grow there continually and regularly. One thing is certain, it is not a miracle; there is some natural explanation for it. And given enough time, science will probably discover how it happens.

Unfortunately, not all anomalies can be so easily distinguished from miracles. For unusualness is not the only characteristic they share with miracles. Some anomalies are also apparently irregular or rare. Eclipses fall into this category, as do earthquakes, tornadoes, and meteors. Here the differentiation from miracles is more difficult but not impossible, at least not in principle. For, while lunar eclipses do not occur regularly, they are naturally predictable. Miracles are not.

---

1. See Norman L. Geisler and Kerby Anderson, *Origin Science* (Grand Rapids: Baker, 1987), chaps. 3–6.

The difficulty in predicting earthquakes is simply a matter of ignorance of all the factors. If all the conditions, both sufficient and necessary ones were known, then seismologists could make exact predictions about earthquakes, as could geologists about volcano eruptions. Thus, natural events are precisely predictable in principle and even (to some degree) roughly predictable in practice.

Furthermore, the basic mechanism of a scientific explanation is knowable, and thus it can be simulated regularly under similar (laboratory) conditions. No such mechanism is knowable for a miracle since it involves a direct act of God in the world. Thus, regularity (a key ingredient of a scientific event) is also present in earthquakes, volcanoes, tornadoes, and other seemingly "irregular" natural events. Regularity is present in principle (by virtue of lab simulation), even though it is not always there in practice in nature. When it comes to miracles, however, neither predictability nor regularity in principle for a human being are even possible, since we cannot know the mind of God. It is for this reason that miracles are distinct from natural anomalies, which are in principle either regular, predictable, or both.

Admittedly, in practice it is not always easy to determine the difference between a mere anomaly and a miracle. Therefore, supernaturalists should not claim any unpredictable event as miraculous unless three conditions hold: (1) it must be an irregular event; (2) it must be at least presently unpredictable; (3) the tell-tale "divine" characteristics must be present. These, as we have seen (chap. 9), include moral and theological factors that give the event its God-like character. In brief, it must bring glory to God and good to the world. Without God's "fingerprints" on it, theists have no right to claim it is miraculous, simply because it is irregular and presently unpredictable.

ANOMALY	MIRACLE
Regular event	Not a regular event
Natural cause	Supernatural cause
Naturally predictable	Not naturally predictable
(in principle)	(even in principle)
Has natural mechanism	Has no natural mechanism
No "divine" characteristics	Has "divine" characteristics

Magic

Miracles differ not only from anomalies; they are also distinguishable from magic. Here we speak not of so-called white magic, black magic, or occult or paranormal activity, but simply of normal illusions, sleight-of-hand, or trickery. The only thing magic has in common with miracles is that both are unusual. Magic is a kind of "wonder." It is amazing to those who do not know the trick. But it has none of the other characteristics of a miracle. In fact, unlike an anomaly, there are known explanations for the magical wonders.[2]

Unlike miracles, magic as such is amoral. It does not bring glory to God, and there are usually no divine truth claims connected with it. If there are supernatural claims connected with magical tricks, they can be exposed by another person who knows the tricks or by scientific tests for the hidden wires or mirrors that create the illusion.

Professional magicians make their living by deceiving. What magicians do can be explained naturally. Of course, there is nothing wrong with magic. It can be very entertaining. When it is mistaken for a miracle, however, it is another matter. Danny Korem, well-known illusionist and investigative reporter, has exposed a number of fraudulent claims to supernatural powers. In his film, *Psychic Confessions,* Korem exposes a famous psychic, James Hydrick, who claimed mental powers to move an object beneath an overturned fish tank on a table. Korem demonstrated that the trick was being done by quietly breathing air on the table. The air moved under the tank and turned the fan wheel inside. On being exposed, the "psychic" confessed his fraud on camera. No transcendent power was involved; it was simply trickery.[3] A former new age warlock, John Anderson, has recently disclosed how he did his so-called new age miracles, including firewalking and psychic surgery.[4]

We expect trickery from magicians and even pay them to do it. The tragedy is when religious leaders use trickery to deceive their followers into believing they have miraculous powers. Jim Jones is a case in point. "People who [supposedly] 'died' and were revived 'miraculously' in the service were Jones' close associates in elaborate

2. For a purely naturalistic explanation of many miracle claims, see Andre Kole, *Miracle and Magic* (Eugene, Oreg.: Harvest House, 1987); Danny Korem, *The Powers* (Downers Grove: Inter-Varsity, 1988).

3. Korem, *Powers.*

4. John Anderson, *Psychic Phenomena—Confessions of a New Age Warlock* (Lafayette, Ind.: Huntington House, 1991), chap. 15.

disguise, each one new for the occasion."[5] These farces were so carefully contrived that even Jones' photographer and his close associates did not realize they were faked. It was later discovered that Jones' bus was filled with makeup, wigs, crutches, and fake cancers. Researcher Mel White adds: "the people needed hope and healing. Through his so-called miracles he gave them both. And the people gave him money and power in return."[6]

Uri Geller claims to have psychic powers. He even convinced some Stanford scientists that he possessed supernormal powers to read minds and bend spoons. But Geller's alleged ESP and mind-reading powers are well known tricks done regularly by good illusionists. And the "scientific" verification of Geller's paranormal powers are open to serious question.

Magician Andre Kole writes about his experience with a so-called psychic surgeon in the Philippines who supposedly performed incisionless operations.[7] To the trained eye of a professional magician, "It didn't take long to discover that the doctor used a very clever form of sleight of hand."[8] According to Kole, the surgeon performed his operations using some of the most clever sleight-of-hand that he had ever seen. Investigation revealed that the psychic surgeon had used coagulated animal blood from his refrigerator. The removed organs were not human but were from chickens, goats, and cows. There was nothing miraculous about it; it was simply clever magic.

Many gurus claim their ability to walk on hot coals is supernatural. But there is a trick to this trip as well. First of all, it is important to get "psyched up" for the walk. Controlling pain is largely a matter of mind-over-matter. Furthermore, it is a known fact that when people move toughened feet quickly over coals (which are poor conductors), they can avoid being burned. Also, not everyone is successful. It takes both courage and skill, and even then some people are burned. Finally, it is important to note that no fire walkers use hot metal, which is a very good conductor of heat. Fire walking is not accomplished by supernormal power. All magic has a perfectly natural explanation once the tricks of the trade are known.

Under close scrutiny, psychic claims lose most of their luster. When F. K. Donnelly, associate professor of history at the University

5. Mel White, *Deceived* (Old Tappan, N.J.: Revell, 1979), p. 42.
6. Ibid., p. 43.
7. Kole, *Miracle and Magic*, pp. 9–10.
8. Ibid., pp. 42–43.

of New Brunswick, reviewed the psychic predictions of psychics in the *People's Almanac* (1975), he discovered that

> Out of the total of 72 predictions, 66 (or 92 percent) were dead wrong. Among the favorites in this category were those that China would go to war with the United States (predicted 4 times) and that New York City would soon be underwater (predicted 3 times). My favorite inept prognostication comes from the Berkeley Psychic Institute, which predicted a war between Greenland and the Soviet Union over fish. Since nuclear weapons were to be used, this was to be very sensibly fought in Labrador in May 1977.[9]

For an alleged supernormal power, this is an abysmal record. As Andre Kole observes, when the psychics are right almost anyone could make similar predictions. For example, one psychic predicted that the United States and Russia would continue to be world powers! The fact that the psychics are sometimes often wrong reveals that they do not possess truly supernatural powers, since God cannot make mistakes.[10]

The "Amazing Randi" has made a living at debunking so-called healers. Randi uncovered the technique by which televangelist Peter Popoff was able to accomplish his apparent supernatural revelations about members of the audience. Randi electronically intercepted the radio messages from the evangelist's wife to a receiver in her husband's ear! She had gathered the information from conversations with the audience before the meeting and later transmitted it to her husband during his healing service. When asked by a Los Angeles television reporter why he employed this method, Popoff replied that he "was told to use this technique by the Holy Spirit."[11] Magician Randi hired a security consultant, Alec Jason, equipped with an electronic scanner who located Popoff's wife on 39:17 megahertz. The transmissions were recorded. One was later played on "The Tonight Show." Popoff repeated exactly what his wife transmitted as though it were coming from God, but it was blatant trickery.

Reports of raising the dead came out of the Indonesian revival reported in 1971. Mel Tari tells of people who were "raised from the dead" in his book, *A Mighty Wind*. When George Peters later went to Indonesia and carefully sifted through the evidence, he con-

9. Ibid., pp. 69–70.
10. It is interesting to note in this connection that one of the tests of a prophet is whether that prophet *ever* gives a false prophecy (see Deut. 18:21–22).
11. Gerald A. Larue, *Free Inquiry* (Fall 1986): 46.

cluded: "I do not doubt that God is able to raise the dead, but I seriously question that He did so in Timor [Indonesia]. In fact, I am convinced that it did not happen."[12]

Peters interviewed people who were allegedly once dead and others who claimed to have raised the dead. He discovered several things. First, "their word for death may mean unconsciousness, coma, or actual death."[13] Second, he found that death in that culture was believed to be in three stages. In the first stage the soul is still in the body. In the second stage the soul is in the home or community. In the third stage the soul goes to the spirit world in the regions beyond. But "not one of the dead persons believed his soul had completely departed to the region beyond." According to the Christian concept of death (the soul leaving the body and going to the spiritual world) none of these people had really died. Third, many of the people who claimed to have died could hear people in the room near their body. Others admitted they were not "totally dead."[14] It seems clear from the evidence Peters uncovered that these people were not really physically raised from the dead but were only reawakened from a coma-like state. They merely went from an unconscious to a conscious state, not from death to life.

To summarize, a miracle can be distinguished from magic in several ways:[15]

MIRACLE	MAGIC
Under God's control	Under human control
Done at God's will	Done at our will
Not repeatable	Repeatable
No deception involved	Deception involved
Occurs in nature	Does not occur in nature
Fits into nature	Does not fit into nature
Unusual but not odd	Unusual and odd

Biblical miracles are unique. First, a miracle is an act of God and, as such, it is under God's control. Hebrews 2:4 tells us that miracles were given "according to his will" (1 Cor. 12:11). Another difference is that miracles cannot be repeated at will. As naturally unre-

---

12. George Peters, *Indonesia Revival* (Grand Rapids: Zondervan, 1973), p. 88.
13. Ibid., p. 89.
14. Ibid.
15. This discussion follows that in Norman L. Geisler, *Signs and Wonders* (Wheaton: Tyndale, 1988), chap. 5.

peatable singularities, they do not occur regularly. While occasionally the same kind of miracle was performed in another context,[16] a prophet did not usually repeat the same miracle over and over. Moses did not have a repeat performance of the exodus. Neither did Joshua do an encore on the sun standing still. On the other hand, magicians can and do repeat their tricks over and over again.

Further, humans do not control the conditions under which miracles occur. Moses certainly did not control the conditions of the great miracle God did through him. Neither did Elijah control the circumstances surrounding God's intervention on Mount Carmel. Mary did not control the factors relating to the miraculous conception of Jesus. But magicians do control the environment. Some kind of control is necessary for the deception to work, and deception is at the heart of their magic.

Another difference between miracle and magic is the latter are odd; they do not really fit into nature. For example, in the natural world rabbits do not come from inside hats but from mother rabbits. Likewise, coins do not appear out of thin air (even though many politicians seem to think so!); they come from mints that get metal from mines. Miracles are not odd; they fit into nature. Jesus' miraculous conception resulted in a natural nine-month pregnancy. He turned water into real wine. In fact, he did immediately what nature does gradually. In this regard, his nature miracles involved a speeding up of natural processes. By contrast to miracle, magic is a misfit. Magic is like a square peg in a round hole. It is odd but not of God.

Mental Cures

Psychosomatic cures happen, but they should not be confused with miracles, even if belief in God is part of the cure.[17] Paul Brand gives evidence that confirms the mind's power to heal the body.

- The mind can effectively control pain. This can be accomplished by simple mental discipline or by "flooding the gates" of the nervous system with distracting noises or additional sensations (e.g., acupuncture).

16. On occasion God did repeat the same kind of miracle. Jesus multiplied loaves twice (Matt. 14:14–21; 25:32–39). The Bible records several raisings of the dead (Matt. 9:18–19; Luke 7:11–15; John 11:17–44). Miracles by nature, however, do not occur regularly, but are naturally unrepeatable events.

17. The discussion here follows Geisler, *Signs and Wonders*, chap. 6.

- In the placebo effect, faith in simple sugar pills stimulates the mind to control pain and even heal some disorders. In some experiments among those with terminal cancer, morphine was an effective painkiller in two-thirds of patients, but placebos were equally effective in half of those! The placebo tricks the mind into believing relief has come, and the body responds accordingly.

- Through biofeedback, people can train themselves to direct bodily processes that previously were thought involuntary. They can control blood pressure, heart rate, brain waves, and even vary the temperature in their hands by as much as 14 degrees.

- Under hypnosis, 20 percent of patients can be induced to lose consciousness of pain so completely that they can undergo surgery without anesthetics. Some patients have even cured their own warts under hypnosis. The hypnotist suggests the idea, and the body performs a remarkable feat of skin renovation and construction, involving the cooperation of thousands of cells in a mental-directed process not otherwise attainable.

- In a false pregnancy, a woman believes so strongly in her pregnant condition that her mind directs an extraordinary sequence of activities: it increases hormone flow, enlarges breasts, suspends menstruation, induces morning sickness, and even prompts labor contractions. All this occurs even though there is no "physical cause"—that is, no fertilization and growing fetus inside.[18]

William Nolen explains that it is a known fact that "neurotics and hysterics will frequently be relieved of their symptoms by the suggestions and ministrations of charismatic healers. It is in treating patients of this sort that healers claim their most dramatic triumphs."[19] In brief, "there is nothing miraculous about these cures. Psychiatrists, internists, G.P.'s, any M.D. who does psychiatric therapy, relieve thousands of such patients of their symptoms every year."[20]

Up to 80 percent of disease is stress-related. Kenneth Pelletier observes that "one standard medical text estimates that 50 to 80 percent of all diseases have their origin in stress."[21] These emotionally

18. Paul Brand, cited in *Christianity Today*, Nov. 23, 1983, p. 19.

19. William Nolen, *Healing: A Doctor in Search of a Miracle* (New York: Random House, 1974), p. 287.

20. Ibid.

21. *Christian Medical Society Journal* (1980).

induced diseases can often be reversed by psychological therapy or "faith healings" where the proper mental attitude brings physical healing.

The mind, however, cannot heal everything. There are some conditions "faith" cannot cure. There are things we can name but we cannot claim. In this category are many organic diseases and death itself. No power of positive thinking can avoid the eventuality of death, raise the dead, see without eyes, grow amputated limbs, or restore those paralyzed by spinal injury. Nolen explains, "Patients that go to a . . . service paralyzed from the waist down as a result of injury to the spinal cord, never have been and never will be cured through [faith-healing]."[22]

Joni Eareckson Tada is a case in point. She became a quadriplegic as the result of a swimming accident. In spite of fervent prayers, she remains unhealed. Joni concludes that "God certainly can, and sometimes does, heal people in a miraculous way today. But the Bible does not teach that He will always heal those who come to Him in faith. He sovereignly reserves the right to heal or not to heal as He sees fit."[23]

Jesus never failed to perform a miracle. Since a miracle is an act of God, it is impossible for it to fail. For "with God all things are possible" (Matt. 19:26). It is true that Jesus did not always attempt to do a miracle (Matt. 13:58). Jesus did not always satisfy the fancy of his audience nor "cast pearls before swine" (Matt. 7:6). But when God attempts a supernatural event he is always successful.

By contrast, psychological attempts to heal are by no means 100 percent successful. In fact, there are many kinds of physical problems that are not curable by a patient's "faith." It has been known for some time that psychological cures are frequent on certain (suggestible) types of personality, such as the hysterionic and hypochondriac. Some studies show that the vast majority of people in the healing movement have these personality types.

Jesus healed a man born blind (John 9) and a man born lame (John 5). The apostles cured a man lame from birth (Acts 3:2). Jesus restored a withered hand (Mark 3:1–5). He calmed the wind (Matt. 8), walked on water (Mark 6), multiplied bread (John 6), and turned water into wine (John 2). Psychological healings do not involve any of these kinds of organic conditions or conditions of nature. They

22. Nolen, *Healing*, p. 286.
23. Joni Eareckson Tada, *A Step Further* (Grand Rapids: Zondervan, 1983), p. 132.

are usually effective only on diseases not involving the loss of bodily organs. Most often they only aid or speed recovery. Never do they instantaneously produce a cure of incurable organic diseases or the restoration of limbs.

Brand states flatly that he had "never yet heard an account of miraculous healing of pancreatic cancer or of cystic fibrosis, or of a major birth defect, or amputation."[24] George Bernard Shaw once caustically commented that the healings at Lourdes, France left him unconvinced because he had seen many crutches and wheel chairs on display but not one glass eye, wooden leg, or toupee.[25]

Jesus healed people "immediately" (Mark 1:42). When he spoke the sea was calmed "completely" (Matt. 8:26). When the apostles healed the man lame from birth, "instantly the man's feet and ankles became strong" (Acts 3:7). Even in the one case of a two-stage miracle, each stage was accomplished immediately (Mark 8:22–25). Miracles produced instantly what nature usually does only gradually. Contrary to biblical miracles, when psychological healings do occur immediately they are on psychosomatic kinds of illnesses. The instantaneous cure of organic and incurable diseases in the name of Christ is a sign of a true miracle (John 9:32).

Although God often calls on the recipient to believe, such belief is not a condition for his being able to perform a miracle. God is in sovereign control of the universe, and he can and does perform miracles with or without our faith. Miracles are done according to his will (1 Cor. 12:11; Heb. 2:4). Jesus performed miracles where there was no faith and even where there was unbelief (Matt. 13:58; 17:14–21). Some recipients could not possibly have believed—they were dead (Matt. 9; Luke 7; John 11). On the other hand, psychological healings require faith on the part of the recipient. Those who suffer from psychosomatic illnesses must believe they can be cured. Whether they believe it is God, a physician, or an evangelist, they must believe to be healed. But there is nothing supernatural about that kind of healing. It happens to Buddhists, Hindus, Roman Catholics, Protestants, and atheists. Healers claiming supernatural powers can do it, but so can psychologists and psychiatrists by purely natural powers and placebo (sugar) pills.

Miracles do not require personal contact. Many whom Jesus never touched were healed. Jesus raised the nobleman's son from the dead

24. Brand, *Christianity Today*, p. 18.
25. Ibid.

from a long distance away (John 4:50–54). Jesus never touched Lazarus when he brought him back to life (John 11:43–44).[26] Jesus performed many other healings for people who were not even present (John 4:49–53). Many faith healings depend on the laying on of hands or some other physical contact or personal influence. Some healers use prayer clothes. Others ask listeners to place their hands on the radio. The personal contact—or at least the psychological build-up—seem to be conditional to the healing itself.

Biblical miracles lasted; there were no relapses. When Jesus healed a disease it did not return. Of course, everyone eventually died, even those he raised from the dead. But this was only as a result of the natural process of mortality, not because the miracle was reversed. When Jesus performed a miracle, it lasted. Whatever other eventual problems the body had, it was not because that miracle did not immediately and permanently repair that particular problem.

On the other hand, psychological cures do not always last. This is true whether they are induced by hypnotism, placebo pills, or faith healers. In fact, not only those "healed" but also the healers have eventually succumbed to bad health.

SUPERNATURAL HEALINGS	PSYCHOLOGICAL HEALINGS
Always immediate	Often not immediate
Don't require personal contact	Often require personal contact
Don't require faith	Require faith
Always successful	Not always successful
Have no relapses	Have many relapses
On all kinds of disease	Not on all kinds of disease
(including organic ones)	(usually only nonorganic ones)[27]

Demonic Signs

The same biblical words used of divine miracles are sometimes used of demonic signs. While these satanic signs are not true miracles, there is no reason to deny they have a supernormal spiritual source. If a miracle is an act of God that brings glory to God and good to the world, then of course a demonic act is not a miracle. On

26. It is true that the apostles laid hands on the Samaritan believers so they might receive the Holy Spirit (Acts 8:18) and speak in tongues (Acts 19:6). The apostles themselves, however, received the Holy Spirit and spoke in tongues without anyone laying hands on them (Acts 2:1–4).

27. See Geisler, *Signs and Wonders*, p. 93.

the other hand, if we are going to believe in acts of God on the basis of the biblical record, then on this same basis we ought to believe that there are evil spirit beings who can perform highly unusual acts that the Bible calls false "signs" and "wonders."

If, then, there are two spiritual sources for unusual "signs" in the world, how can we tell them apart? In brief, God's signs are God-like, and Satan's signs are Satan-like. More specifically, the answer involves several "tests" (1 John 4:1) that the believer is urged to apply, all of which amount to saying that satanic "signs" have satanic (evil) characteristics and divine miracles have God-like (good) characteristics. Numerous evil indicators are mentioned in the Bible, such as idolatry (1 Cor. 10:20), immorality (Eph. 2:2), divination (Deut. 18:10), false prophecies (Deut. 18:22), occult activity (Deut. 18:14), worshiping other gods (Deut. 13:1–2), deceptive activity (2 Thess. 2:9), contacting the dead (Deut. 18:11–12), messages contrary to those revealed through true prophets (Gal. 1:8), and prophecies that do not center on Jesus Christ (Rev. 19:10; see also Matt. 5:17; Luke 24:27; John 5:39; Heb. 10:7). And, as with any other counterfeit and deception, we must know the characteristics of good and evil and then look carefully to see which are connected with the unusual event.

Whenever there was any serious question in the Bible as to which events were of God, a contest followed in which good triumphed over evil by an even greater miracle than the magic or satanic signs. In the contest between Moses and the Egyptian magicians, they could not reduplicate the sign of turning dust into life and gave up: "This is the finger of God" (Exod. 8:18–19). In the dispute between Moses and Korah the earth opened up and swallowed Korah and company and the dispute ended abruptly (Num. 16). Elijah triumphed over the false prophets of Baal on Mount Carmel when fire came from heaven and consumed the water-soaked sacrifices (1 Kings 18). In the New Testament, Jesus and the apostles triumphed over evil spirits and even exorcised them.

When necessary, the supreme God proves himself supreme. Only God is infinite in power; Satan is finite in power. Only God can create life and raise the dead. At best Satan only counterfeits attempts to do so. Satan is the master magician and the superscientist. With his vast knowledge and deceptive ability he is able to convince many that he can do what God does, but he cannot. Only God can suspend the natural laws he has made. At best Satan can only utilize natural laws in ways that may appear at times to be violating God's laws. God never relinquishes his sovereign control of the universe; Satan only

works by God's permission (Job 1:10–12). In brief, a true miracle
and a satanic sign differ in the following ways:

DIVINE MIRACLE	SATANIC SIGN
Supernatural	Supernormal
By an infinite spiritual power	By a finite spiritual power
Connected with truth	Connected with error
Associated with good	Associated with evil
Never associated with the occult	Often associated with the occult
Always successful	Not always successful

Acts of Special Providence

Not all "acts of God" are miracles. In nature God acts regularly;
through miracles he acts rarely. But not all rare acts are miracles.
There are also anomalies and special acts of providence. The latter is
like an anomaly of nature in that it is an unusual event within nature.
That is, it happens only rarely. Likewise, neither anomalies nor special providence involve an exception to any natural laws, such as
walking on water, turning water into wine, and raising the dead.
God simply uses his knowledge of nature in such a way as to accomplish unusual events for his purposes.

God is active in general providence by his sustenance of the natural world. It is God who sends the rain, makes the grass grow, and
feeds his creatures (Ps. 104). General providence is simply a theological way of describing how God works through natural laws. Or,
more properly, what we call "natural laws" involve the way God
works regularly in his creation.

God also works through special providence, which is different
from both general providence and miracles. Unlike general providence, there is something unusual about a special act of providence.
It does not happen every day, and when it does it makes us sit up
and take notice. On the other hand, a special act of God's providence is not a miracle. The most crucial difference is that a miracle is
never the product of a natural law, but special providence is. Special
providence simply utilizes natural laws to produce an unusual effect.

Another way to state the difference is that special providence is
accomplished by God's prearranging of natural events, but a miracle
is a direct intervention into the natural world. A miracle, then,
involves God's direct action in the world in a special way, whereas
in special providence God acts only indirectly through natural laws.

For example, Jesus walking on water was a miracle, but the fog at Normandy (during the landing of Allied troops in World War II) was a special act of God's providence. Without the cover of fog, the troops would have suffered heavy casualties and possibly Hitler's tyranny would not have been overthrown. But while the Allied troops walked through the protecting fog, none of them walked on the water.

Much of what we call miracles in common parlance is simply God's special providence. Most legitimate healings in response to prayer fit into this category. There may be other "spontaneous recessions" of the same illness where no prayer was given. Nonetheless, if the event is rare enough and the timing is significant enough, it may very well be a special act of God's providence. But in such a case, God superseded no natural law but simply used his infinite knowledge to preplan things in such a way as to bring about this truly amazing event.

Of course, from a spiritual perspective, it matters little how God accomplishes his unusual feats—whether by miracles or special providence. He nevertheless deserves the praise. We should not overclaim. A special answer to prayer is just that—a special answer to prayer. We should not exaggerate the situation by placing it on the same level as the miracles of Jesus and the apostles. The Bible says the apostles had special "signs" (2 Cor. 12:12) that God gave them for a special purpose (Acts 2:22; Heb. 2:3–4). The differences can be outlined as follows:

MIRACLE	SPECIAL PROVIDENCE
Natural law is superseded	Natural law is not superseded
Goes beyond nature	Works through nature
Divine intervention in nature	Divine prearranging of nature
God's direct activity in the world	God's indirect activity in the world

All That Glitters Is Not Gold

Not everything unusual is supernormal (anomalies are a case in point). Neither is everything abnormal really supernormal. Some unusual events have a psychological cause, not a supernatural cause. Furthermore, some of what is taken for miracle is just plain magic. More careful scrutiny, however, reveals some clear distinctions between unusual events, with their purely natural explanations, and truly supernatural events.

The fact that some people are deceived into believing that some unusual but purely natural events are supernatural in no way proves that no genuine miracles have ever occurred. It may be that the presence of counterfeits points to the existence of the authentic. This does not, however, prove that genuine miracles exist today any more than contemporary counterfeit Rembrandts prove that Rembrandt is still painting. It merely indicates that there once were authentic ones. Certainly, distinguishing false claims from genuine ones will add credibility to any attempt to establish an authentic miracle. What we do know is that God can perform miracles. Whether he ever has is the subject of the next chapter.

 **12**

ARE MIRACLES ACTUAL?

Its verification, even in the case of a fresh miracle, is essentially
one involving the historical method with its reliance on direct
witnesses, on direct observation, and circumstantial evidence.
—Stanley Jaki

THUS FAR WE HAVE DISCUSSED the possibility of miracles. The antisupernaturalist's charges have been examined and found lacking.
Miracles have not proven to be either impossible or incredible.
Miracles have not been shown to be either unscientific or unidentifi-
able. Further, biblical miracles in particular are not mythological but
historical. Neither can miracles be ruled out as nonessential to
Christianity or undefinable. Miracles are unusual but they are not
antinatural. This does not mean, of course, that all miracle claims are
true. Nonetheless, if God exists, then miracles are possible because
of his control over the world. And they are definable in terms of his
character manifest in the world.

Objections Against Miracles

Miracles are possible, but are they actual? Granting the context of
a theistic universe that makes miracles possible and identifiable, can
an event be identified as a miracle? Or, if God exists, what (if any)
event known to fit the earmarks of a miracle has actually occurred?
Since the focus here is on New Testament miracles that occurred in
the first century, this raises the question of the credibility of the New

Testament documents and witnesses. Both of these were seriously challenged by Hume.

Hume offers two arguments against the witnesses to miracles. The first rules out testimony to miracles in principle. This argument would eliminate belief in miracles in advance of looking at the evidence. Since we have already shown (chap. 2) that a priori attempts to eliminate miracles have failed, our concern here is with Hume's a posteriori argument. The second says that in practice there is not enough evidence to establish New Testament miracles.

First, says Hume, "there is not to be found, in all history, any miracle attested by a sufficient number of men of such unquestioned good-sense, education, and learning as to secure us against all delusion in themselves." Nor are there enough witnesses of "such undoubted integrity, as to place them beyond all suspicion of any design to deceive others." Neither are they "of such credit and reputation in the eyes of mankind, as to have a great deal to lose in case of their being detected in any falsehood." Finally, neither have the alleged miracles been "performed in such a public manner and in so celebrated a part of the world as to render the detection unavoidable."[1]

Second, our knowledge of human nature renders miracle stories suspect. "We may observe in human nature a principle which, if strictly examined, will be found to diminish extremely the assurance which we might, from human testimony, have in any prodigy." Just "the strong propensity of mankind to the extraordinary and marvelous . . . ought reasonably to beget suspicion against all relations of this kind." And "if the spirit of religion join itself to the love of wonder, there is an end of common sense."[2]

Third, says Hume, "it forms strong presumption against all supernatural and miraculous relations that they are observed chiefly to abound among ignorant and barbarous nations." And "if a civilized people has ever given admission to any of them, that people will be found to have received them from ignorant and barbarous ancestors." Further, "the advantages are so great of startling an imposture among ignorant people that . . . it has a much better chance for succeeding in remote countries than if the first scene had been laid in a city renowned for arts and knowledge."[3]

1. David Hume, *An Inquiry Concerning Human Understanding*, ed. C. W. Hendel (New York: Bobbs-Merrill, 1955), 10.2.124.
2. Ibid., 10.2.125–26.
3. Ibid.,10.2.126–28.

Hume sums it all up in these words: "Upon the whole, then, it appears that no testimony for any kind of miracle has ever amounted to a probability, much less to a proof." Further, "even supposing it amounted to a proof, it would be opposed by another proof derived from the very nature of the fact which it would endeavour to establish."[4]

Even though Hume's argument appears to imply that he is really open to the actual evidence for or against a miracle, it turns out that he has ruled out in advance the credibility claims for any miracle.

First, Hume admits that no amount of witnesses would convince him of a miracle. Speaking of what he acknowledges to be highly attested Jansenist miracles of his day, Hume writes: "And what have we to oppose to such a cloud of witnesses but the absolute impossibility or miraculous nature of the events which they relate?" And this, Hume adds, "surely, in the eyes of all reasonable people, will alone be regarded as a sufficient refutation."[5] So, no matter how many witnesses to these "absolutely impossible" events, no "reasonable person" will believe them. If this is the case, then Hume is still approaching every miraculous event, no matter how well it is attested, with an incurably naturalistic bias. All the talk of testing the credibility of witnesses is a poorly concealed disguise for an intractable antisupernaturalism.

Second, Hume's sword cuts both ways. One can also argue that knowledge of human nature reveals that there are also biases against accepting miracles. Hume himself reveals this bias at times. This is evident in the passage just cited where he concluded: "And what have we to oppose to such a cloud of witnesses but the absolute impossibility or miraculous nature of the events which they relate?" Taken at face value this would mean that no matter how many good witnesses were produced for a miracle, Hume would still reject it. What is this but an antisupernaturalistic bias against miracles—a skeptical human tendency no less entrenched than the propensity of others to accept almost anything unusual as supernatural?

Third, Hume is inconsistent. He allows no testimony for miracles, and yet he allows testimony of those who have seen water frozen in preference to the testimony of those who never have. But why allow testimony for one event and not for the other, unless it is simply a matter of prejudice against miracles? He cannot reply that it is because others have seen water frozen over and over again, for this

4. Ibid., 10.2.137.
5. Ibid., 10.2.133.

begs the question. The problem is that a tropical jungle tribe has never seen it, so why should they accept the testimony of outsiders who say they have, regardless of whether they have seen it more than once. Miracles have happened more than once. Further, according to Hume's own principles, even if we saw water freeze only once and walked or slid on it, that would be sufficient to know that it happened. But, the same applies for miracles, and only an antisupernatural bias would hinder a person from accepting reliable testimony about its occurrence.

Fourth, Hume is apparently unaware of the strong historical evidence for the reliability of the New Testament documents and witnesses. At least, he overlooks it. But New Testament miracles cannot be dismissed without taking a closer look at them. For no one should rule out the possibility of these miracles in advance of looking at the evidence for them.

The Evidence for New Testament Miracles

There are two basic questions to answer before we can know if New Testament miracles actually occurred. The first is the reliability of the New Testament documents, and the second the integrity of the witnesses.

There is more documentary evidence for the reliability of the New Testament than for any other book from the ancient world. Some of the great classics from antiquity survive in only a handful of manuscript copies. According to the great Manchester scholar F. F. Bruce, we have about nine or ten good copies of Caesar's *Gallic Wars*, twenty copies of Livy's *Roman History*, two copies of Tacitus's *Annals*, and eight manuscripts of Thucydides' *History*.[6] The most documented secular work from the ancient world is Homer's *Iliad*, which survives in some 643 manuscript copies. By contrast, there are now over 5,366 Greek manuscripts of the New Testament.[7]

The New Testament has earlier manuscripts. One of the marks of a good manuscript is its age. Generally the older the better, since the closer to the time of original composition, the less likely it is that the text has been corrupted. Most books from the ancient world survive not only in a handful of manuscripts but in manuscripts that were

6. F. F. Bruce, *The New Testament Documents: Are They Reliable?* (Grand Rapids: Eerdmans, 1965), p. 16.

7. See Norman L. Geisler and William. E. Nix, *A General Introduction to the Bible,* rev. ed. (Chicago: Moody, 1986).

written about one thousand years after they were originally composed. (It is rare to have, as the *Odyssey* does, one manuscript copied
only five hundred years after the original.) The New Testament, by
contrast, survives in complete books from a little over 150 years after
the books were composed. And one fragment survives from within
about a generation of the time it was composed.[8] No other book
from the ancient world has as small a time gap (between composition and earliest manuscript copies) as the New Testament.

It is also safe to say that the New Testament is the most accurately
copied book from the ancient world. There is widespread misunderstanding about the so-called errors in the biblical manuscripts. Some
have estimated there are about 200,000 of them. First, these are not
really "errors" but only variant readings, the vast majority of which
are strictly grammatical. Second, these readings are spread throughout more than 5,300 manuscripts, so that a variant spelling of one
letter of one word in one verse in 3,000 manuscripts is counted as
3,000 "errors." Third, these 200,000 variants represent only some
10,000 places in the New Testament. Fourth, only 1/60th of these
variants rise above "trivialities." This would leave a text 98.33 percent pure.[9]

The great scholar A. T. Robertson said that the real concern is
only with a "thousandth part of the entire text." This would make
the New Testament 99.9 percent free of significant variants. The
noted historian Philip Schaff calculated that, of the 150,000 variants
known in his day, only 400 affected the meaning of the passage, only
50 were of real significance, and not even one affected "an article of
faith or a precept of duty which is not abundantly sustained by other
and undoubted passages, or by the whole tenor of Scripture teaching."[10]

To illustrate how a copyist's error does not affect either substan-
tial meaning or message, note the following telegrams, one received
one day and the other the next.

"Y#U HAVE WON A MILLION DOLLARS."

"YO# HAVE WON A MILLION DOLLARS."

Even if we received only the first telegram we know what the message is in spite of the error. And if we received twenty telegrams,
each one of which had a similar mistake in a different place, we

8. This fragment is the John Rylands Papyri (P52), dated A.D. 114.
9. Geisler and Nix, *General Introduction*, pp. 473–75.
10. Ibid., p. 474.

would say that the message is beyond all reasonable doubt. Now it is
noteworthy that the New Testament manuscripts have a smaller per-
centage of significant copyist errors than this telegram. Further, with
over 5,300 manuscripts (compared to a few lines), the real message
of the New Testament is no more affected than is the message of the
telegram.

By comparison with the New Testament, most other books from
the ancient world are not nearly so well authenticated. The well-
known New Testament scholar Bruce Metzger estimates that the
Hindu *Mahabharata* is copied with only about 90 percent accuracy
and Homer's *Iliad* with about 95 percent. By comparison, he estimates the New Testament is about 99.5 percent accurate.[11] So, by
even conservative standards, the New Testament survives in the
reconstructed text with about 99 percent accuracy and 100 percent
of the basic message coming through. In fact, "The number of
manuscripts of the New Testament, of early translations from it, and
of quotations from it in the oldest writers of the Church, is so large
that it is practically certain that the true reading of every doubtful
passage is preserved in some one or other of these ancient authorities. This can be said of no other ancient book in the world."[12]

Tracing manuscripts back to the first century does not prove, of
course, that those who wrote them were either honest or accurate.
In order to establish the authenticity of what the manuscripts say,
we must examine the evidence relating to the witnesses.

To begin with, the New Testament claims to be composed by
eyewitnesses. Most (if not all) of the New Testament claims to be
written by eyewitnesses and contemporaries of the events of Jesus'
ministry (ca. A.D. 29–33). Matthew is written by an observer who
gives long and direct quotes from Jesus (see 5–7; 13; 23; 24–25).
He was accustomed to taking records as a tax collector (9:9). Mark
was a disciple of Peter (1 Pet. 5:13) and an eyewitness of Christ (2
Pet. 1:16). Luke was an educated contemporary of Christ who said
that just as those who from the beginning were eyewitnesses and ser-
vants of the word (the apostles), so too it seemed fitting for him as
well to write it out in consecutive order (Luke 1:1–3). John the
apostle was a direct eyewitness (John 21:24; cf. 1 John 1:1), as was
Peter (2 Pet. 1:16). Paul was a contemporary of Christ and a witness

11. Bruce Metzger, *Chapters in the History of New Testament Textual Criticism*
(Grand Rapids: Eerdmans, 1963).

12. Frederic Kenyon, *Our Bible and the Ancient Manuscripts*, 4th ed. (New York:
Harper, 1958), p. 55.

of his resurrection (1 Cor. 15:8). Paul lists many others who saw the resurrected Christ, together with a group of over five hundred, most of whom were still alive when he wrote (1 Cor. 15:6).

The evidence that these claims should be taken at face value is weighty. First, there is the general rule of historical research expressed by Kant. This rule says in effect that historical reports are "innocent until proven guilty." That is, what purports to be authentic would be accepted as authentic, until it is shown to be unauthentic. As Kant points out, this is indeed the rule used in the normal discourses of life. Were the opposite used, there would be a breakdown of everyday communication.

Second, there is what is known in law as the "ancient document rule." According to this rule, "a writing is sufficiently authenticated as an ancient document if the party who offers it satisfies the judge that the writing is thirty years old, that is unsuspicious in appearance, and further proves that the writing is produced from a place of custody natural for such a document." In fact, "Any combination of circumstances sufficient to support a finding of genuineness will be appropriate authentication."[13] Now, using this rule, the New Testament should be considered authentic. It is an ancient document whose transmission can be traced and whose custodianship has been proper. In fact, many great legal minds have been convinced of the truth of Christianity on the basis of the rules of evidence used to try life-and-death cases in the courtroom. In point of fact Simon Greenleaf, a professor of law at Harvard who wrote a book on legal evidence, was converted to Christianity in just this way.[14] Using the canons of legal evidence he concluded that "Copies which had been as universally received and acted upon as the Four Gospels, would have been received in evidence in any court of justice, without the slightest hesitation."[15]

Third, there is the early dating of the New Testament manuscripts. The most knowledgeable scholars date the New Testament books within the lifetime of the eyewitnesses and alleged authors. Archeologist Nelson Glueck wrote, "We can already say emphatically that there is no longer any solid basis for dating any

13. *McCormick's Handbook of the Law of Evidence*, 2d ed. (St. Paul, Minn.: West, 1972), sec. 223.
14. See John W. Montgomery, *The Law above the Law* (Minneapolis: Bethany, 1975).
15. Simon Greenleaf, *The Testimony of the Evangelists: Examined by the Rules of Evidence Administered in Courts of Justice* (Grand Rapids: Baker, 1965), pp. 9–10.

book of the New Testament after about A.D. 80."[16] The renowned
paleographer William F. Albright declared that "every book of the
New Testament was written by a baptized Jew between the forties
and the eighties of the first century A.D. (very probably between
about A.D. 50 and 75)."[17] More recently, even the radical "death-
of-God" theologian Bishop John Robinson became honest with the
facts and declared that the New Testament was written by contemporaries only seven years or so after the events and were circulated
among other eyewitnesses and/or contemporaries of the events.[18]

Fourth, the science of archeology has confirmed the historical
accuracy of the Gospel records. This can be dramatically illustrated
through the writings of Sir William Ramsay, whose conversion from
a skeptical view of the New Testament was supported by a lifetime
of research in the Near Eastern world.

> I began with a mind unfavorable to it [Acts], for the ingenuity and
> apparent completeness of the Tubingen theory had at one time quite
> convinced me. It did not lie then in my line of life to investigate the
> subject minutely; but more recently I found myself often brought in
> contact with the book of Acts as an authority for the topography,
> antiquities, and society of Asia Minor. It was gradually borne in upon
> me that in various details the narrative showed marvelous truth.[19]

Ramsay discovered that Luke was a first-rate historian. In Luke's
references to thirty-two countries, fifty-four cities, and nine islands
there are no errors! Luke's narration of the life and miracles of Christ
must likewise be accepted as authentic. And since Luke's narration
of Christ's life and miracles accord with that of the other Gospels,
we have here an archeological confirmation of the Gospels that
record the miracles and resurrection of Christ. In brief, from a
strictly historical point of view, we could not have better evidence
for the authenticity of events than we possess for the events in the
life of Christ recorded in the New Testament.

The great miracle of Christianity is the death and resurrection of
Christ. If these events are true, all other New Testament miracles are
easily believable. Indeed, in many respects the resurrection is the cor-

16. Nelson Glueck, *Rivers in the Desert: A History of the Negev* (Philadelphia:
Jewish Publication Society, 1969), p. 136.
    17. Interview with William F. Albright, *Christianity Today*, Jan. 18, 1963, p. 359.
    18. See John A. T. Robinson, *Honest to God* (Philadelphia: Westminster, 1963).
    19. William Ramsay, *St. Paul the Traveller and the Roman Citizen* (New York:
Putnam, 1896), p. 8.

nerstone miracle of Christianity. The apostle Paul is willing to concede that "if Christ has not been raised, our preaching is useless and so is your faith" (1 Cor. 15:14). In fact, Jesus used his resurrection as a proof of his deity (Matt. 12:40; John 2:19; 20:28). Christianity stands or falls on this event. If it is true, then it substantiates what Jesus claimed to be: God. If it is false, then not only is Christianity false but so is the claim for the miraculous resurrection of Christ. How sufficient are the witnesses?

Hume outlines the basic criteria that he believes necessary for testing the credibility of witnesses: "We entertain suspicion concerning any matter of fact when the witnesses contradict each other, when they are but few or of a doubtful character, when they have an interest in what they affirm, when they deliver their testimony with hesitation, or with too violent asseverations [declaration]."[20]

Basically, these can be translated into four questions: (1) Do the witnesses contradict each other? (2) Are there a sufficient number of witnesses? (3) Were the witnesses truthful? (4) Were they nonprejudicial? Let us apply Hume's tests to the New Testament witnesses for the resurrection of Christ.

Do the witnesses contradict each other? The answer is: the testimony of the witnesses is not contradictory. Each New Testament writer tells the crucial and overlapping part of the whole story. Christ was crucified around A.D. 33 under Pontius Pilate in Jerusalem. He claimed to be the Son of God and offered miracles in support of that claim. He was crucified and confirmed to be dead and buried. Yet three days later the tomb was empty. Further, to many groups of people on many occasions over the next month or so, Jesus physically appeared in the same body that had died. He proved his physical reality to them so convincingly that these skeptical men boldly preached the resurrection a little over a month later in the same city, whereupon thousands of Jews were converted to Christianity.

To be sure, there are minor discrepancies in the Gospel accounts. One account (Matt. 28:5) says there was one angel at the tomb; John says there were two (John 20:12). But two things should be noted about these kinds of discrepancies. First, they are conflicts but not contradictions. That is, they are not irreconcilable. Matthew does not say there was *only* one angel there; that would be a contradiction. The simple rule of harmony is this: "Where there are two, there is one." Second, conflict of testimony is just what we might expect

20. Hume, *Inquiry*, 10.1.120.

from authentic, independent witnesses. Any perceptive judge who
heard several witnesses give identical testimony would discount their
testimony, assuming they were in collusion.

Are there a sufficient number of witnesses? There are twenty-seven
books in the New Testament. These books were written by some
nine different persons, all of whom were eyewitnesses or contemporaries of the events they recorded. Of these books, six are crucial to
the topic of New Testament miracles (Matthew, Mark, Luke, John,
Acts, 1 Corinthians). All of these books bear witness to the miracle
of the resurrection. Further, even critical scholars now acknowledge
that these books are first-century documents, most of which were
written before A.D. 70, while contemporaries of Christ were still
alive. Virtually all scholars acknowledge that 1 Corinthians was written by the apostle Paul around A.D. 55 or 56, only about two
decades after the death of Christ. This is a powerful witness to the
reality of the miracle of the resurrection for several reasons. First, it is
a very early document, written only about twenty-two years after the
event occurred. Second, it is written by an eyewitness of the resurrected Christ (1 Cor. 15:8; cf. Acts 9). Third, it provides a list referring to over five hundred eyewitnesses of the resurrection (1 Cor.
15:6). Fourth, it contains a reference to the fact that most of these
witnesses were still alive (v. 6).

Were the witnesses truthful? Few challenge the fact that the New
Testament provides one of the greatest standards of morality known
to humankind in Jesus' emphasis on love (Matt. 22:36–37) and in
the Sermon on the Mount (Matt. 5–7). His apostles repeated this
same teaching in their writings (see Rom. 13; 1 Cor. 13; Gal. 5).
Furthermore, their lives exemplified their moral teaching. Most of
them even died for what they believed (2 Tim. 4:6–8; 2 Pet. 1:14),
an unmistakable sign of their sincerity.

In addition to teaching that truth is a divine imperative (Rom.
12:9), it is evident that the New Testament writers were scrupulous
about expressing it in their writings. Peter declares: "We did not follow cleverly invented stories" (2 Pet. 1:16). The apostle Paul insists
"Do not lie one to each other" (Col. 3:9). Where the New
Testament writers' statements overlap with the discovery of histori-
ans and archeologists, they have proven to be accurate. Noted archeologist Nelson Glueck concludes, "It may be stated categorically that
no archaeological discovery has ever controverted a Biblical reference. Scores of archaeological findings have been made which confirm in clear outline or exact detail historical statements in the

Bible."[21] Millar Burrows notes that "more than one archaeologist has found his respect for the Bible increased by the experience of excavation in Palestine."[22] In fact, there is no proof that the New Testament writers ever lied in their writings or deliberately falsified the facts of the case. If they were asked in court "to swear to tell the truth, the whole truth, and nothing but the truth" their testimony would be accepted as valid by any unbiased jury in the world. In brief, their testimony shows absolutely no sign of perjury.

Were the witnesses prejudiced? There is every reason to believe that New Testament witnesses of the miracles of Christ, particularly of his resurrection, were not predisposed to believe the events to which they gave testimony. First, the apostles themselves were predisposed not to believe the testimony of others that Christ had risen from the dead. When the women reported it, "their words seemed to them like nonsense" (Luke 24:11). Even when some of the disciples saw Christ themselves they were "slow of heart to believe" (Luke 24:25). Indeed, when Jesus appeared to ten apostles and showed them his crucifixion scars, "they still did not believe it because of joy and amazement" (Luke 24:41). And even after they were convinced by Jesus' eating food, their absent colleague Thomas protested that he would not believe unless he could put his finger in the scars in Jesus' body (John 20:25).

Second, Jesus not only appeared to believers; he also appeared to unbelievers. He appeared to his unbelieving half-brother, James (John 7:5; 1 Cor. 15:7). Indeed, he appeared to the greatest unbeliever of the day—a Jewish Pharisee named Saul of Tarsus (Acts 9). If Jesus had only appeared to those who were either believers or with the propensity to believe, then there might be some legitimacy to the charge the witnesses were prejudiced. But just the opposite is the case.

Third, the witnesses to the resurrection had nothing to gain personally for their witness to the resurrection. They were persecuted and threatened with death for their stand (see Acts 4, 5, 8). As a matter of fact, most of the apostles were martyred for their belief. Certainly, it would have been much more profitable personally for them to deny the resurrection. Rather, they proclaimed and defended it in the face of death.

21. Glueck, *Rivers in the Desert*, p. 31.
22. Millar Burrows, *What Mean These Stones?* (New Haven, Conn.: American Schools of Oriental Research, 1941), p. 1.

Fourth, to discount their testimonies because they believed in the resurrected Christ is like discounting an eyewitness of a murder because he actually saw it occur! The prejudice in this case is not with the witnesses but with those who reject their testimony.

One Last Objection to Miracles Considered

Hume offers one more argument against miracles. He insists that, even if miracles actually occurred, they would have no value as evidence for the truth of a religious system.

Hume claims that "every miracle, therefore, pretended to have been wrought in any of these religions (and all of them abound in miracles) . . . so has it the same force, though more indirectly, to overthrow every other system" and "in destroying a rival system, it likewise destroys the credit of those miracles on which that system was established." In short, since a miracle's "direct scope is to establish the particular system to which it is attributed, so has it the same force . . . to overthrow every other system."[23] Miracles, being all of the same kind, are self-cancelling as witnesses to the truth of a religious system.

Rather than being a disproof of New Testament miracles, Hume's argument unwittingly supports the authenticity of biblical miracles. We may restate his argument this way:

1. All non-Christian religions (which claim miracles) are supported by similar "miracles" claims.
2. But such "miracles" have no evidential value (since they are self-cancelling and based on poor testimony).
3. Therefore, no non-Christian religion is supported by miracles.

If this is so, then we can argue that only Christianity is divinely confirmed as true.

1. Only Christianity has unique miracle claims confirmed by sufficient testimony.
2. What has unique miraculous confirmation of its claims is true (as opposed to contrary views).

23. Hume, *Inquiry*, 10.2.129–30.

3. Therefore, Christianity is true (as opposed to contrary views).

The support for the uniqueness of Christian miracles has already been presented (chap. 11). No other world religion has verified miracles like those in the New Testament. Jesus' miracles were instantaneous, always successful, and unique. So-called miracle workers who claim partial success effect only psychosomatic cures, engage in trickery, perform satanic signs, or other naturally explainable events. In fact, no contemporary healer even claims to be able to heal all diseases (including "incurable" ones) instantaneously, with 100 percent success. But Jesus and his apostles did. This is unique, and it sets these miracles against all other supernatural claims of any other religion.

Historical evidence by its very nature is uncoercive, but it can be persuasive. Indeed, the case for the authenticity of New Testament miracles is very strong. Compared to other events from the ancient world, the grounds for accepting the authenticity of the documents and the reliability of the witnesses are superior. In fact, it is safe to say that were it not for the miraculous nature of the events recorded therein (and the moral implications thereof) that few would reject the truthfulness of the New Testament accounts on historical grounds.

But neither, as we have seen, should the New Testament miracle stories be rejected on philosophical grounds. If a theistic God exists, then there is no reason to rule out the possibility of miracles. As for the actuality of miracles, past or present, this can be determined only on the basis of the evidence. And the evidence points strongly in favor of accepting the New Testament miracles as authentic. And since no other religion offers like miracles, only Christianity is miraculously confirmed to be true. In short, we have good evidence to believe that Jesus died for our sins and rose from the grave for our justification before God (Rom. 4:25). Thus, we can trust him when he declares, "I am the way and the truth and the life" (John 14:6), and no one comes to the Father except through him.

THE HISTORICITY
OF OLD TESTAMENT MIRACLES

IN A VERY POPULAR BOOK on miracles,[1] C. S. Lewis argues strongly for the authenticity of New Testament miracles but strangely relegates Old Testament miracles to the realm of myth. This is due in part to his critical views on the Old Testament but more specifically to his unique view that in Christ myth became history. This, however, is clearly contrary to both the recording of these events in the Old Testament and the teaching of the New Testament, which refers to these Old Testament events as historical.

First, Old Testament miracles fit the monotheistic concept of God that permeates the entire Old Testament record. A theistic God by nature is a miracle-working God. Since he is a God beyond the world who created the world, he is involved in supernatural acts from the very first verse of the Bible. Furthermore, since this theistic God is loving and cares for the world, it is understandable that he would want to intervene in it on behalf of his creatures. In the Old Testament record miracles fit perfectly with its central message about God who is the ultimate object of all its themes.

Second, the miracle stories come to us as part of the same historical record from which we know the other events that are known to be a part of real space-time history. There is absolutely no evidence that any manuscripts existed without these miracles in them. They

---

1. C. S. Lewis, *Miracles* (New York: Macmillan, 1947), p. 139.

are present in the very oldest manuscripts we possess without the slightest recorded statement to the contrary.

Third, the miracles of the Old Testament are an integral part of the history it records and the message it conveys. Take away the miraculous events of Genesis 1–2, for example, and the message about the Creator evaporates with it. Likewise, the story of Noah and his faithfulness to God in a day of violence and unbelief makes no sense apart from God's intervention to save him and destroy the world by a flood. And Israel's call of God and special deliverance from Egypt is meaningless apart from the supernatural intervention by which these things were accomplished. The same is true of the miracles of Elijah, Elisha, and Jonah. Each is an inseparable part of the very fabric of history they record.

Fourth, the New Testament reference to Old Testament miracles verifies their historical nature. This is supported in numerous instances.

The creation of the world is not only repeatedly cited in the New Testament but the events and persons involved are taken to be historical. Adam and Eve are referred to as historical figures (Matt. 19:4; Rom. 5:12; 1 Cor. 11:8–9; 15:45; 1 Tim. 2:13–14). The Romans passage is unmistakable: it is through one man that sin entered the world and thus death by sin, and thus death spread to all people. What could be clearer: we die physically because a physical Adam sinned and brought physical death on himself and all his posterity. The New Testament takes the literal creation of Adam and Eve so historically that Adam is even listed as the first name in Jesus' genealogy (Luke 3:38). Likewise, Adam is called "the first man Adam" in direct comparison to Christ who is the "last Adam" (1 Cor. 15:45).

The authenticity of many of the supernatural events in the Old Testament are used as the basis for New Testament teaching. For example, Jesus based the truth of his resurrection on the fact of Jonah's miraculous preservation in the belly of a great fish, saying, "For just as Jonah was three days and three nights in the belly of the sea monster, [even] so shall the Son of Man be three days and three nights in the heart of the earth" (Matt. 12:40 NASB). The strong contrast ("just as"), the emphatic manner in which it is cited, and the important historical truth with which it was associated (the resurrection of Christ) all reveal that Jonah's deliverance was not a myth. Given the context, it is inconceivable that Jesus meant something like: "Just as you believe that mythology about Jonah, I would like to tell you about the historicity of my death and resurrection." The same is true about Jesus' reference to the historicity of Noah and the flood, saying, "[even] so shall the coming of the Son of Man be" (Matt. 24:39 NASB).

Jesus referred to numerous miraculous Old Testament events as historical, including the creation of the world (Matt. 24:21), the creation of Adam and Eve (Matt. 19:4), the flood (Matt. 24:39), the miracles of Elijah (Luke 4:26), Jonah in the great fish (Matt. 12:40), and the supernatural prediction of Daniel (Matt. 24:15).

In brief, in view of Jesus' use of the Old Testament miracles, there is no way to challenge their authenticity without impugning his integrity. So accepting New Testament miracles as authentic, while rejecting those of the Old Testament, is inconsistent.

Finally, there is nothing more incredible or unbelievable about Old Testament miracles than those in the New Testament. In fact, once the existence of a theistic God is granted, then all miracles become possible. As C. S. Lewis himself noted, "If we admit God must we admit miracle? Indeed, indeed, you have no security against it."[2] As a matter of fact, the greatest miracle of all—the resurrection of Christ—occurs in the New Testament. If this is historical, then there is no reason to reject the miracles of Moses, Elijah, or Elisha, which were lesser by comparison.

2. Ibid., p. 109.

SUPERNATURAL EVENTS
IN THE BIBLE

Passage	Description
Genesis	
1	Creation of the world.
5:19–24	Translation of Enoch to be with God.
7: 9–12, 17–24	The Noahic flood.
11:1, 5–9	The judgment on the tower of Babel.
12:10–20;	Plagues on Pharaoh for taking Abraham's wife.
17:15–19; 18:10–14	
19:9–11	Angels blind the Sodomites.
19:15–29	The destruction of Sodom and Gomorrah.
19:24–26	Lot's wife turned to salt.
21:1–8	Sarah's conception of Isaac.
Exodus	
3:1–15	The burning bush.
4:1–5	Moses' rod turned into a serpent and back.
4:6–7	Moses' hand becomes leprous and is restored.
7:10–12	Aaron's rod turns into a serpent and swallows up the rods of the Egyptian sorcerers.
7:19–24	Water in Egypt turned into blood.
8:5–7; 12–13	Frogs are brought forth on the land of Egypt.
8:16–18	Lice are brought forth on the land of Egypt.

8:20–24	Swarms of flies are brought forth on Egypt but not on the land of Goshen.
9:1–7	Murrain (deadly pestilence) is brought on the cattle of the Egyptians, but not on Israel's cattle.
9:8–11	Ashes produce boils on the Egyptians but not on Israel's men and animals.
9:22–26	A terrible storm of thunder, hail, and fire which ran along the ground.
10:3–19	A plague of locusts on the Egyptians.
10:21–23	A plague of darkness was brought on the Egyptians while Israel had light.
12:29–30	Slaying the firstborn children.
13:21–22	The pillar of cloud led Israel by day, and the fire led them by night.
14:19–20	The angel of the Lord protects Israel from the Egyptians.
14:21–29	The parting of the Red Sea.
15:23–25	Sweetening of the bitter waters of Marah.
16:12–13	The camp of Israel is covered with quail.
16:14–15	Manna is provided for Israel to eat.
17:5–6	Moses strikes the rock and water is provided.
17:8–16	Remarkable victory over Amalek.
19:16–18	Fire and smoke engulf Mount Sinai.
19:19–25	God answers Moses from the Mount.
20:1–17	God gives the Ten Commandments to Moses.

Leviticus

| 9:23–24 | Fire from the Lord consumes the burnt offering. |
| 10:1–7 | The fatal judgment upon Nadab and Abihu. |

Numbers

11:1–2	Fire from God to consume murmuring Israelites.
12:10–15	Miriam is made leprous and is healed.
16:28–33	Korah and his rebels are swallowed by the earth.
16:35	Fire from the Lord consumes 250 men who offered incense.
16:46–48	The plague stopped by the offering of incense.
17:8	Aaron's rod buds.
20:7–11	Moses strikes the rock to bring forth water.
21:6–9	Healing by looking at the brass serpent.
22:21–35	Balaam's donkey speaks.

Joshua

| 3:14–17 | The waters of the Jordan are divided. |

5:13–15	The appearance of the captain of the Lord's hosts.
6	The fall of Jericho.
10:12–14	The sun stands still upon Gibeon.

Judges

2:1–5	The Angel of the Lord appears to Israel.
3:8–11	The Spirit of the Lord comes upon Othniel.
3:31	Shamgar slays six hundred Philistines with an ox-goad.
6:11–24	The Angel of the Lord appears to Gideon.
6:36–40	The sign of Gideon's fleece.
7:15–25	God delivers Midian into the hands of Gideon.
13:3–21	The Angel of the Lord appears to Manoah.
14:5–6	Samson slays the young lion.
15:14–17	Samson slays the Philistines with the jawbone of a donkey.
16:3	Samson tears down the city gate and carries it away.
16:27–31	Samson causes the collapse of the temple of Dagon.

1 Samuel

3:2–10	The voice of God calling Samuel.
5:1–5	The overturning of the god, Dagon.
5:6–12	Philistines in Ashdod smitten with tumors.
6:19	The Lord smites the men of Beth-Shemesh.
28:15–20	Samuel appears from the dead to rebuke Saul.

2 Samuel

6:6–7	The Lord fatally smites Uzzah.

1 Kings

3:3–28	God gives Solomon great wisdom.
17:1	Elijah prays and rain does not come for three years.
17:2–6	Elijah is fed by the ravens.
17:8–16	Meal and oil are supplied for the widow of Zarephath.
17:17–24	Elijah raises the widow's son.
18:17–38	Fire from heaven consumes the sacrifice of Elijah on Mount Carmel.
18:41–46	Elijah prays and God sends an abundance of rain in response.
19:5–8	Elijah is fed by the Angel of the Lord.

2 Kings

1:9–15	Fire from heaven consumes two captains and their men.
2:7–8	Elijah parts the waters of the Jordan and walks across on dry ground.
2:11	Elijah is taken up into heaven in a chariot of fire.
2:13–14	Elisha parts the waters of the Jordan.
2:19–22	Elisha heals the waters of Jericho.
2:24	Blasphemous youths killed by she-bears.
3:15–20	Ditches are mysteriously filled with water.
4:1–7	A widow's oil pot is refilled with oil by God.
4:8–17	Elisha prophesies and the Shunammite woman bears a son.
4:32–37	Elisha raises the Shunammite's son.
4:38–41	Elisha detoxifies the poisonous pottage.
4:42–44	One hundred men are abundantly fed with twenty loaves of bread and twenty ears of corn.
5:1–14	Naaman is healed of leprosy.
5:27	Gehazi is struck with leprosy.
6:5–7	Iron axe head floats on water.
6:16–17	Elisha's servant's vision of the mountain full of horses and chariots of fire.
6:18	The Syrian army is struck with blindness.
6:19–20	God opens the eyes of the Syrians after Elisha leads them into Samaria.
13:20–21	A dead man is raised by contact with Elisha's bones.
20:9–11	Ahaz's sundial turns backward by ten degrees.

Job

38–42:6	God speaks to Job from the whirlwind.

Isaiah

1:1	Isaiah's vision concerning Jerusalem.
6	Isaiah's vision of the Lord.

Ezekiel

1	Ezekiel has a vision of God's glory.

Daniel

2:26–45	Daniel recounts and interprets Nebuchadnezzar's dream.

3:14–30				Three Hebrew youths delivered from the fiery furnace.
5:5				The handwriting on the wall.
6:16–23				Daniel saved from the lions.
7:1–8:14				Daniel's visions.
9:20–27				Daniel's vision of the seventy weeks.
10:1–12:13				Further visions of Daniel.

Jonah

1:4–16				Tempestuous storm from God to arrest the fleeing Jonah.
1:17				The Lord prepares a great fish to swallow Jonah.
4:6				The Lord prepares a gourd to shade Jonah.
4:7				The Lord prepares a worm to smite the gourd.
4:8				The Lord prepares a vehement east wind.

Matthew	Mark	Luke	John	Description
		1:11–19		An angel of the Lord appears to Zacharias.
		1:20–22		Zacharias is struck dumb.
		1:26–38		Angel of the Lord appears to Mary.
		1:64		Zacharias healed of dumbness.
		2:9–15		Angels appear to shepherds.
3:16–17	1:9–11	3:21–23		Holy Spirit descended as a dove, and a voice from heaven spoke.
4:11	1:13			Angels minister to Jesus after the temptation.
			1:42–48	Jesus sees Nathanael under the fig tree.
			2:1–11	Water turned into wine.
			2:23	Jesus performs many signs.
			4:46–53	Nobleman's son healed.
		4:30		Jesus escapes from the hostile crowd.
		5:6		Catching a draught of fish.
	1:23–25	4:33–35		Casting out an unclean spirit.
8:14–15	1:30–31	4:38–39		Healing Peter's mother-in-law.
8:16	1:32–34	4:40		Healing many sick people.

Matthew	Mark	Luke	John	Description
4:23–24	1:39			Jesus heals all manner of sickness and casts out many demons.
8:2–3	1:40–42	5:12–13		Cleansing a leper.
9:2	2:3–5	5:18–20		Healing a paralytic.
			5:6–9	Healing an infirmed man at Bethesda.
12:9–13	3:1–5	6:6–10		Healing the man's withered hand.
12:15	3:10			Healing of many people.
8:5–13		7:1–10		Healing a centurion's servant.
		7:11–15		Raising a widow's son at Nain.
12:22				Casting out a demon from a blind mute.
8:23–26	4:35–39	8:22–24		Stilling the storm on the sea of Galilee.
8:28–32	5:6–13	8:28–33		Casting out the demons and allowing them to enter swine.
9:23–25	5:35–42	8:49–55		Raising the ruler's daughter.
9:20–22	5:25–34	8:43–48		Healing the woman with an issue of blood.
9:27–30				Healing two blind men.
	6:5			Jesus heals a few sick people in Nazareth.
9:32–33				Casting out a demon from a deaf mute.
9:35				Jesus heals the sick in many cities.
14:14				Jesus heals the sick among the great multitude.
14:15–21	6:35–44	9:10–17	6:5–13	Feeding the five thousand.
14:25	6:48		6:19	Walking on the sea.
14:35–36	6:55–56			Healing of many at Gennesaret.
15:21–28	7:24–30			Healing the Canaanite woman's daughter.
	7:31–35			Healing a deaf mute.
15:30–31				Jesus heals many among a great multitude.
15:32–38	8:1–8			Feeding the four thousand.

Matthew	Mark	Luke	John	Description
	8:22–25			Healing a blind man at Bethsaida.
17:1–8	9:2–8	9:28–36		Jesus' transfiguration.
17:14–18	9:17–27	9:38–42		Healing the epileptic boy.
17:24–27				Temple tax in the fish's mouth.
			9:1–7	Healing a man born blind.
		11:14		Curing a demon-possessed, blind mute.
		13:11–13		Healing an infirmed woman.
		14:2–4		Healing a man with dropsy.
			11:43–44	Raising Lazarus.
		17:12–14		Cleansing ten lepers.
19:1–2				Jesus heals many at the borders of Judea.
20:30–34				Healing the two blind men.
21:14		18:35		Jesus heals the blind and the lame man in the temple.
21:18–19	11:12–14; 20			Withering the fig tree.
			12:28–29	A voice from heaven.
		22:51		Restoring a servant's ear.
27:51	15:38	23:45		The veil of the temple is torn from top to bottom.
27:51				A great earthquake, and the rocks broken.
27:52–53				The tombs opened and many of the dead are raised.
28:1–10	16:1–8	24:1–12	20:1–9	The resurrection of Jesus.
28:1–7				An angel rolls the stone from the grave and speaks to the women.
28:5–8	16:5–7	24:4–8		Angelic appearance to those at the sepulcher.
			20:11–13	Two angels appear to Mary.
	16:9		20:14–17	Jesus appears to Mary Magdalene.
28:9–10				Jesus appears to the women.
	16:12	24:13–35		Jesus appears to the two on the road to Emmaus.
			20:19–23	Jesus appears to ten apostles.
28:16–20	16:14–18	24:36–49	20:26–31	Jesus appears to eleven apostles.
			21:1–25	Jesus appears to seven apostles.
			21:6	Miraculous catch of fish.

Passage	Description

Acts

Passage	Description
1:3–5	Jesus appears to all the apostles.
1:6–9	Jesus ascends into heaven.
1:10–11	Two angels appear to the apostles.
2:1–4	The coming of the Holy Spirit on the apostles.
2:4–13	The apostles speak with other tongues.
3:1–11	Peter heals the lame man in the temple.
5:5–10	Ananias and Sapphira are killed.
5:12	Many signs and wonders performed by the apostles.
5:18–20	Angel releases the apostles from prison.
7:55–56	Stephen sees Jesus at the right hand of God.
8:7	Unclean spirits are cast out of many.
8:13	Philip performs miracles and signs.
8:14–17	The Samaritans receive the Holy Spirit.
8:39-40	Philip caught away by the Holy Spirit.
9:3–7	Jesus appears to Saul (cf. 1 Cor. 15:8).
9:10–16	Jesus appears to Ananias.
9:17–19	Saul's sight is restored.
9:32–34	Peter heals Aeneas.
9:36–42	Dorcas is restored to life.
10:1–8	Cornelius receives a vision.
10:9–16	Peter receives a vision three times.
10:44–48	Cornelius' household receives the Holy Spirit.
12:7–10	An angel releases Peter from prison.
12:23	The angel of the Lord kills Herod.
13:8–11	Elymas the sorcerer is blinded.
14:8–10	Paul heals a lame man at Lystra.
16:16–18	Paul casts a demon out of a young woman.
16:25–26	Prison doors opened and Paul's and Silas' bands are broken off.
18:9–10	The Lord appears to Paul.
19:6	Believers at Ephesus receive the Holy Spirit.
19:11–12	Many unusual signs performed by Paul.
20:9–12	Eutychus is restored to life.
23:11	The Lord appears to Paul.
28:3–6	Paul protected from the viper bite.
28:7–8	Paul heals the father of Publius.

1 Corinthians

Passage	Description
15:6	Jesus' appearance to five hundred people.
15:7	Jesus' appearance to James.

2 Corinthians

12:1–6	Paul's vision of heaven.

Revelation

1:1–3:22	John's vision of Jesus.
4:1–22:21	John's vision of the future.
6:12	A great earthquake.
6:12	The sun becomes black as sackcloth.
6:12	The moon becomes as blood.
6:13	The stars fall from heaven to earth.
6:14	Every mountain is moved out of its place.
8:7	Hail and fire mingled with blood falls on the earth.
8:8	Something like a great burning mountain is cast into the sea, and a third part of the sea becomes blood.
8:9	A third part of the creatures in the sea die.
8:9	A third part of the ships are destroyed.
8:10–11	A great, burning star falls from heaven and a third part of the rivers and fountains become bitter.
8:12	A third part of the sun is darkened.
8:12	A third part of the moon is darkened.
8:12	A third part of the stars are darkened.
9:1	A star falls from heaven.
9:2	The sun is darkened by the smoke from the bottomless pit.
9:3–11	A plague of locusts are given power to torment men for five months.
9:18	A third part of mankind is killed.
11:5	The two witnesses devour their enemies by fire from their mouths.
11:6	The two witnesses stop the rain for 3 1/2 years.
11:6	The two witnesses turn water into blood.
11:6	The two witnesses smite the earth with many plagues.
11:11	The two witnesses are raised from the dead.
11:12	The two witnesses ascend into heaven.
11:13	There is a great earthquake in which a tenth part of the city falls, and seven thousand men are slain.
11:19	There are lightenings, voices, thunderings, earthquake, and great hail.
16:2	Foul and loathsome sores fall on men who worship the beast.

16:3	The sea becomes as blood, and every living soul in it dies.
16:4	The rivers and fountains of waters become blood.
16:8	The sun scorches men with fire.
16:10	Darkness covers the kingdom of the beast.
16:12	The water of the river Euphrates is dried up.
16:18	There are voices and thunders and a great earthquake.
16:20	The islands flee and the mountains cannot be found.
16:21	A great hail of heavy stones falls on people.
18:1–24	The fall of Babylon.
19:11–16	The return of Jesus Christ.
21:1	The new heaven and the new earth appear.
21:10	The new Jerusalem descending from heaven.

* Not all these events are miracles in the technical sense of a direct action of God superseding a natural law. Some (e.g., Gen. 7, 19) may be a special act of divine providence where God uses natural laws to accomplish his purpose (see chap. 11).

ANNOTATED BIBLIOGRAPHY

Aquinas, Thomas. *Summa contra Gentiles.* 3.98–103.
  Aquinas defends the strong concept of miracle as a violation of natural law. This is perhaps the best representation of classic theism's view of the miraculous.
Augustine. *City of God.* 21.6–8; 22.8–10.
  The classic statement of the view that miracles are irregular exceptions to the regular patterns of nature.
Bube, Richard, ed. *Journal of American Scientific Affiliation.* December 1978, several articles.
  A good interchange by J. W. Montgomery and the Basinger brothers on the apologetic value of miracles.
Campbell, George. *A Dissertation on Miracles.* 1762. Reprint. London: T. Tegg and Son, 1834.
  This is a reply to David Hume by a famous Scottish theologian of his day.
Clarke, Samuel. *The Works of Samuel Clarke.* Vol. 2. London, 1738.
  In this book Clarke answers the objection to miracles arising out of the philosophies of Hobbes and Spinoza.
Jaki, Stanley. *Miracles and Physics.* Front Royal, Va.: Christendom, 1989.
  Jaki provides a good survey of the relation of miracles to modern physics, arguing strongly for the miraculous based on the validity of our physical senses.
Jividen, Jimmy. *Miracles: From God or Man?* Abilene, Tex.: ACI Press, 1987.
  This is a clear, strong analysis of the nature and purpose of every miracle in the New Testament. It concludes that all biblical miracles are authentic and all postbiblical miracle claims are not.
Lewis, C. S. *God in the Dock.* Grand Rapids: Eerdmans, 1970.
  This book contains several excellent and insightful chapters on miracles.
_____. *Miracles.* New York: Macmillan, 1947.
  This is the best overall apologetic for miracles written in this century.
Morison, Frank. *Who Moved the Stone?* Grand Rapids: Zondervan, 1976.

A converted skeptic who had sought to disprove the miracle of the resurrection has written this unique defense of the event.

Paley, William. *A View of the Evidences of Christianity.* "Prefatory Considerations," 1794.

A classic eighteenth-century response to the deistic denial of miracles.

Smart, Ninian. *Philosophers and Religious Truth.* London: SCM, 1964, chapter 2.

This contribution is a significant response to the criticism that miracles are unscientific.

Swinburne, Richard. *The Concept of Miracle.* London: Macmillan, 1989.

One of the best philosophical defenses of miracles written in this generation.

————, ed. *Miracles.* New York: Macmillan, 1989.

One of the best collections of articles by important scholars on both sides of the issue.

Tennant, F. R. *Miracle and Its Philosophical Presuppositions.* Cambridge: Cambridge University Press, 1925.

This is an important work by the late Cambridge philosopher of religion who gives a rational defense of miracles and of the supernatural in the Anglican tradition.

Warfield, B. B. *Counterfeit Miracles.* New York: Scribner, 1918.

This book argues strongly for biblical miracles and against miracles after the apostolic period.

Whately, Richard. *Historical Doubts Relative to Napoleon Bonaparte.* New York: Robert Caster, 1849.

Whately satirizes David Hume's famous attack on miracles, claiming that Hume's views would eliminate historical knowledge of other unique (nonmiraculous) events of the past.

INDEX OF TOPICS

INDEX OF PERSONS